Yorkshi

Murders, Mansl
Madness & Exe

Paul Chrystal

Stenlake Publishing Ltd.

Text © Paul Chrystal, 2018.
First published in the United Kingdom, 2018,
by Stenlake Publishing Ltd.
Telephone: 01290 551122
www.stenlake.co.uk

Printed by Berforts, 17 Burgess Road, Hastings, TN35 4NR

ISBN 9781840338201

About the Author

Paul Chrystal is the author of 100 or so books, many of which are about Yorkshire. He is a regular contributor to a number of history magazines, is reviewer for *Classics for All*, writes for a national daily newspaper, and has appeared on the BBC World Service, Radio 4's PM programme and various BBC local radio stations in York, Manchester, Cleveland and Sheffield.

By the Same Author

The Place Names of Yorkshire
Wheels Around Yorkshire
Old Yorkshire Country Life
York Churches and Other Places of Worship
York and Its Railway

www.paulchrystal.com

Title page: George Bishop scything down his father (see page 35). *Illustrated Police News.*

Introduction

As a mark of respect for relatives of victims and perpetrators, this book only includes murders and executions up to 1945.

Be that as it may, the book features 168 murders, manslaughters and executions which occurred in the county of Yorkshire from the 1623 up to 1945. It includes cases of husbands killing wives and wives killing husbands; parents killing babies and children; children killing parents; strangers killing strangers and people being killed by people known to them. These cases include murder by poison, murder by blunt instrument and murder by sharp weapon; they involve decapitation, suffocation, mutilation and sexual depravity. The second part of the book examines subjects relating to murder: infanticide, arsenic and other poisons. Other topics cover Yorkshire jails and hangmen, houses of correction, body snatching, legislation relating to murder and manslaughter, insanity, puerperal depression, mercy and pardons, gallows, gibbets and scaffolds, and forensic science.

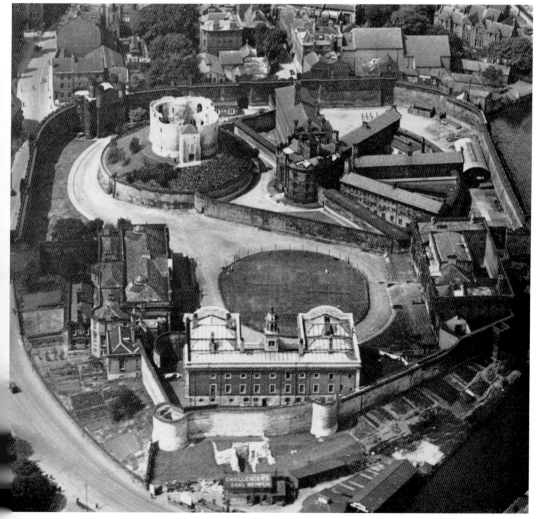

York Castle and prison from the air.

Part One: Murders & Executions

Ralph Raynard 1623

This story of murder and gibbeting is well told by Charles George Harper in *The Great North Road* published in 1901. Here is an adaptation: The "White House" was the scene of a murder in 1623. At that time the innkeeper was a certain Ralph Raynard, who "kept company" with a "young lusty" girl in service at Red House, Thornton Bridge. The lovers quarrelled, and in a pique the girl married a farmer named Fletcher, of Moor House, Raskelf. Unhappily, she did not love the man she had married, while she certainly did retain an affection for her old sweetheart "in unlawful lust", and he for her. Going between Raskelf and Easingwold on market-days on her horse, she would often stop at the "White House" and chat with Ralph Raynard; the ostler, Mark Dunn, minding the horse when she dismounted. Raynard's sister kept house with him at the inn, and she saw that no good could come of these visits, but he would not listen to her warnings, and the visits continued. It was not long before Fletcher's neighbours began to hint to him something of these little flirtations of his wife with her old lover; and one evening he caught the ostler of the "White House" in his orchard, where he was waiting for an opportunity to deliver a message from Raynard to her. The man returned to the inn without having fulfilled his mission, and smarting from a thrashing he had received at the hands of the indignant farmer. Shortly after this, Fletcher had occasion to go a journey. Things had not been going well with him, and his home was rendered unhappy by the evidence of his wife's dislike of him. Little wonder that he had dismal forebodings as he set out. Before leaving, he wrote on a sheet of paper: "If I should be missing, or suddenly wanted be, mark Ralph Raynard, mark Dunn, and mark my wife for me", addressing it to his sister.

No sooner was he gone than Mrs. Fletcher mounted her horse and rode to Raskelf, where, with Raynard and Mark Dunn, a murderous plot was contrived for putting Fletcher out of the way. They were waiting for him when he returned at evening, and as he stood a moment on Dawnay Bridge, where the little river runs beneath the highway, two of them rushed upon him and threw him into the water. It would be difficult for a man to drown here, but the innkeeper and the ostler leapt in after him, and as he lay there held his head under water, while his wife seized his feet. When the unfortunate man was quite dead they thrust his body into a sack, and, carrying their burden with them to the inn, buried it in the garden, Raynard sowing some mustard-seed over the spot. The lovers continued their wicked course of lust and drunkenness, his wife explaining Fletcher's absence to his fleeing from some writs served on him. The murder had taken place 1st of May. On 7th July, Raynard went to Topcliffe Fair, and put up at the "Angel". Going into the stable, he was confronted by the apparition of the unhappy Fletcher, glowing with a strange light and predicting retribution. He rushed out among the booths, and tried to think he had been mistaken. Coming to a booth where they sold small trinkets, he thought he would buy a present for his sweetheart, and, taking up a chain of coral beads, asked the stall keeper how it looked on the neck. To his dismay the apparition stood opposite, with a red chain round its neck, with its head hanging to one side, like that of an executed criminal, while a voice informed him that presently he and his accomplices should be wearing hempen necklaces.

When night fell he mounted his horse and rode for home. On the way, at a spot called the Carr, he saw something in the road. It was a figure emerging from a sack and shaking the water off itself, like a Newfoundland dog. With a yell of terror the haunted man dug his heels into his horse and galloped madly away; but the figure, irradiated by a phosphorescent glimmer and dragging an equally luminous sack after it, was gliding in front of him all the while, at an equal pace, and so continued until the "White House" was reached, where it slid through the garden hedge and into the ground where Fletcher's body had been laid.

Raynard's sister was waiting for him, with supper ready, and with a dish of freshly cut mustard. She did not see the spectre sitting opposite, pointing a minatory finger at that dreadful salad, but he did, and, terrified, confessed to the crime. Sisterly affection was not proof against this, and she laid information against the three accomplices before a neighbouring justice of the peace, Sir William Sheffield of Raskelf Park. They were committed to York Castle, tried, and hanged on July 28th, 1623. The bodies were afterwards cut down and taken to the inn, being gibbeted near the scene of the crime, on a spot still called Gallows Hill, where the bones of the three malefactors were accidentally ploughed up a hundred years ago.

Old Wife Green 1630

In 1630 Old Wife Green was burnt at the stake in Pocklington's market place for being a witch – the last such burning in England. Even more interesting, though, was Isabella Bilington who was found guilty in 1649 of crucifying her mother at Pocklington. She later sacrificed a calf and a chicken and was hanged along with her accomplice husband.

Elizabeth and Helen Drysdale 1647

It only took 90 minutes for Robert Boss of Heslington and Robert Blanchard of Walmgate to die from oxalic acid poisoning administered by their girlfriends Elizabeth and Helen Drysdale aged 26 and 24 respectively at the home of Dame Robinson at the Sign of the Maypole in Clifton. The acid was bought earlier that day at chemist William Brooks in Stonegate, York. The two men forgave the women before they expired but they were hanged at St. Leonard's, meeting their end with 'more than womanly fortitude'. Any motive went with them to the dissecting room.

George and Maria Merrington 1649

Congestion caused by the huge crowds was always a problem at York hangings, not least in the case of George and Maria Merrington hanged for the murder of William Rex of Dunnington whose body they concealed in a shallow grave in their kitchen. The Merringtons were hanged at St. Leonard's, Green Dykes, outside Walmgate Bar but the journey to the gallows was fraught, due to the great number of people thronging the streets as they passed by in a cart guarded by dragoons. In Fossgate one woman had her leg broken in the melée and one man fractured his thigh bone. In Walmgate the Merringtons fainted but were revived by a glass of mint water, fortified by a glass of wine provided by the landlady of the Golden Barrel. Their bodies were given to surgeons for dissection after the hanging.

Thomas Haley – late 17th century

Batley carpenter Thomas Haley was 47 when he was murdered; his wife was 26; she was having an affair with a younger man. Haley was beaten to death and then his body was concealed under a manure heap and later moved to a place called Clark's Pit where it was discovered by police bloodhounds.

John 'Swift Nick' Nevison 1684

Think of highwaymen and York and the name of Dick Turpin immediately springs to mind. We should not, however, forget, John Nevison (1639-1684), also known as William Nevison, one of Britain's most notorious highwaymen, and a gentleman rogue to boot. He was nicknamed Swift Nick by King Charles II after his impressive 200-mile dash from Kent to York to establish an alibi for a robbery he had committed earlier that day. At dawn one day in 1676 witnesses saw Nevison commit a robbery in Gad's Hill near Rochester. Fifteen hours later he arrived in York's Museum Gardens on horseback and engaged the Lord Mayor, who was playing bowls, in conversation. His alibi thus established, Swift Nick was acquitted of the charges against him.

Nevison was born in Wortley, Barnsley and operated between Huntington and York on the Great North Road. Spoils between him and his accomplices were divided up in the Talbot Inn in Newark. Nevison never resorted to violence, was always polite, and only robbed the rich.

He was, nevertheless, beyond rehabilitation and was later tried and convicted for the theft of a horse and highway robbery at York assizes in 1677. He was locked up in York Castle where his leg irons weighed 28 pounds but was pardoned and was to be transported when he offered to inform against his accomplices. In 1681 he was taken from York to be enlisted in a penal company of soldiers posted to Tangier but escaped. He was re- arrested on 6th March 1684 at the Three Houses Inn in Sandal Magna near Wakefield and tried for the murder of Darcy Fletcher, a police constable who had tried to arrest him near Howley Hall at Soothill in Batley. Nevison was taken back to York where, because he had breached his pardon, was told "he must dye, for he was a terrour to the country". Nevison was hanged at the Knavesmire in March 1684 and buried in an unmarked grave in St. Mary's Church, Castlegate.

William Smith 1753

When William Smith – a farmer at Great Broughton near Stokesley – learned that his widowed mother was to marry Thomas Harper of Ingleby Manor he was most displeased; his inheritance would be diluted at least, evaporated at worst. The only option was to poison Thomas Harper and restore his own place in the pecking order.

While out one day buying some equine medicine a voice in his head told him to buy some arsenic as well – for the rats of course. The arsenic ended up in a cake which was consumed not just by Harper but, even more tragically, by his two children as well. All three died. Smith was soon apprehended when he returned from hiding in Liverpool to the scene of the crime. Smith hanged and his body sent for dissection.

Eugene Aram 1759

Eugene Aram was born at Ramsgill in Nidderdale in 1704; he moved to Knaresborough in 1734 and set up a school at the top of High Street, in White Horse Yard, now Park Square. A self-educated scholar and linguist, Aram was familiar with Latin and Greek, Celtic and Hebrew as well as with advanced mathematics. Things took a turn for the worse though when Aram was implicated in a fraudulent scheme along with a flax-dresser, Richard Houseman, and a young cordwainer, Daniel Clark.

On February 7th 1744 Clark disappeared; it was assumed that he had absconded with some valuables. Aram paid off his debts and left Knaresborough. However, that was not the end of the matter: in August 1758, a skeleton was unearthed on Thistle Hill. Houseman, accused of Clark's murder, denied that the remains were Clark's – 'this is no more Clark's bone than it is mine' and eventually confessed that Clark was, in fact, buried in St. Robert's Cave by the river; Houseman alleged that he had seen Aram strike Clark. Aram was traced to King's Lynn, where he was an usher in a school; he was arrested and brought back and imprisoned in York Castle. A sophisticated defence speech failed to save him and he was found guilty at York Assizes; on August 6th 1759, he was sentenced to swing in York, and later hung on the gibbet in Knaresborough, near the Mother Shipton Inn. Body parts were stolen as relics.

Two writers made Eugene Aram well known to the Victorians – Thomas Hood, in *The Dream of Eugene Aram: Murderer* (1831), which vividly describes his guilty conscience, and Edward George Bulwer (Lord) Lytton in a work of pure fiction, *Eugene Aram*, which attempts to exonerate him. The 1875 *Memoirs of the Celebrated Eugene Aram With the "Gleamings" After Eugene Aram Unexpectedly Gathered After the Publication of His "Memoirs"*, by Norrisson Cavendish Scatcherd and Thomas Hood, introduces a disaffected, and hard-up, Mrs. Aram to the witness box; she was also infatuated with Houseman: 'until her pecuniary resources failed her, she was mute; and then, after some grumbling, she turned the full tide of her wrath on her unfortunate husband. Her gossip, from the account we have of it, was that of a faithless, incredible, and frivolous woman. As to the murder, she could, at most, only speak from suspicion'.

George Harger 1762

Harger was found guilty of the murder of John Moore of Kirby Malzeard. He hanged at York Castle but not before he mounted an unsuccessful attempt to tunnel out of the prison using a knife and a shoemaker's hammer. He was found underground and was then chained to the wall along with three accomplices while waiting execution.

Joseph Hogg 1768

The garrisoning of soldiers in Low Harrogate must have galvanised the growth of inns here. The Hoggs, landlords of the Bell, certainly quartered soldiers – in 1768 Joseph Hogg was falsely accused of murdering someone who may have been a soldier. *The York Courant* tells us that the evidence was based entirely on 'the distempered brain of a woman' who, it is careful to tell readers, was many years ago 'big with bastard child'.

John Scott 1774

John Scott already had a son by his common law wife, Hannah Stocks and the last thing he wanted was another mouth to feed. The couple lived at Northhowram near Halifax. And so when he discovered that Hannah was pregnant again he tried to get her to take an abortifacient; when she refused, he forced her to ingest arsenic at knifepoint. Scott hanged at the Knavesmire and his body was given over for dissection.

Elizabeth Boardingham 1776

When Elizabeth Boardingham's smuggler husband was locked up in York Castle she took a lover, Thomas Aikney, and when her husband was released she openly lived in adultery with Aikney for three months before she decided that her husband should be eliminated. Aikney was less than keen but, when fuelled with drink, finally agreed to murder him. The plan was that Elizabeth would continue to live with her husband in York but that she would awaken him one night so that he could investigate an alleged intruder, Aikney. Aikney intruded as planned: he stabbed Mr. Boardingham in the thigh and stomach but then lost his nerve and fled, leaving the knife in the wound: Boardingham staggered out of the house bleeding. One account tells of neighbours finding 'in one hand the bloody instrument that he had just drawn out of his body, and the other supporting his bowels, which were dropping to the ground'.

Aikney was hanged for murder and his body sent to Leeds Infirmary for dissection. Elizabeth Boardingham was strangled and burnt at the stake for petit treason for planning the murder. Her ashes were sold as souvenirs. Petit treason was the crime committed by a servant in killing his or her master, by a wife in killing her husband, or by an ecclesiastic in killing his superior. Petit treason was not abolished until 1790.

Frank Fearne 1782

Frank Fearne was a Sheffield apprentice. One day he visited Nathan Andrews, a watchmaker, armed with a knife and a pistol. Fearne shot Andrews in the back then knifed him before smashing his skull in. Fearne was found with some of the watchmaker's watches in his possession and was duly arrested. Hanging and post-mortem dissection were deemed too good for Fearne so he was sentenced to the gibbet at Loxley Edge after hanging; carrion then proceeded to eat his rotting flesh. Live gibbeting involved placing the condemned alive in a metal cage and left to die of thirst, after which they would be pecked and picked at by the birds. After 25 years of acting the deterrent, Fearne's skeleton was finally taken down from the gibbet.

Catherine Foster 1784

Catherine Foster poisoned her husband, John Bayston, a farm labourer in Easingwold north of York. She had her eye set on Richard Brown – and John was in the way. Foster later maintained that she had been planning to poison Bayston for some time, but it was only after an argument that she determined to give him arsenic. She was found to be insane; had she been convicted she would have burned at the stake for petit treason.

Alcohol and Long Street, Easingwold, sometimes did not mix, it seems: Tom Cowling died from excessive drinking at the Royal Oak in 1825 and William White, a joiner, suffered the same fate when he carelessly downed a pint of rum instead of ale in The Unicorn. Thomas Gill tells us that at The New Rose & Crown Frank Sellars 'writhing under the anguish of disappointed love in his ardent attachment to Miss Fanny Thorpe, a pretty dressmaker in the town, hung himself in the coach house' (*Gill's Family Almanack*, 1872). In 1838 a lovelorn Mary Scaife from Ripon hanged herself in the kitchen of The New Inn; a verdict of temporary insanity was returned.

Ann Scalbird 1794

Ann Scalbird has the expertise and thoroughness of the medical profession to thank for the accurate diagnosis she received post-mortem and the subsequent conviction of her daughter-in-law for poisoning her with arsenic in Batley. Small consolation indeed for the excruciating painful and slow six day death Mary had to endure, but consolation all the same. This happened in the time before reliable tests had been discovered for arsenical poisoning. The doctors in attendance were George Swinton of Dewsbury and Benjamin Sykes of Gomersall, a graduate of Guy's Hospital Medical School in London, a centre of excellence even then. Swinton crucially elected to forego the usual practice of a quick autopsy on the victim's kitchen table and called in Sykes so that they could do a proper job.

Jane Hostler and Elizabeth Beal 1799

Long Riston is a village midway between Hull and Beverley; it was the home of little Thomas Hostler, his mother and father William and Jane, and his aunt, Elizabeth Beal. The three adults had been savagely abusing Thomas over a long period of time; in fact so bad was it that four nieighbours felt it necessary to take out a recognizance against the abusers, so confident were they that their action would succeed and they would not lose their £30 (each) deposit. The assize records spoke of beatings with 'hands and feet and staves and sticks' on every part of Thomas's naked body leading to 'large and grievous wounds, swellings and bruises'. In short, the toddler was beaten to within an inch of death, until, finally, his parents' sadistic actions killed him. The women were recorded as being guilty of murder, along with William Hostler; his entry, though, was mysteriously amended to not guilty. No one knows why. The women were transported to Van Dieman's Land via the pillory and a dungeon in York Castle.

Mary Thorp 1800

Mary Thorp went into service aged fourteen: she was affable and well-liked by all, not least by her employers. Sadly though she was relentlessly stalked and pursued by an admirer who was 'to bring her to ruin, misery and disgrace…he at length succeeded in his diabolical aim, ruined and left her'. Mary became 'a miserable mother' and in a frenzied moment a week after the birth took the baby to a pond, weighed her down with a stone around its neck and threw her into the water. That at least is what the papers reported; in actual fact Mary went with the baby to Ecclesfield near Sheffield, strangled the baby with some tape and then threw her in the river near Bridge Houses.

Mary was charged with the murder of her illegitimate daughter at York; she pleaded not guilty to murder; the defence was that she had acted when she was delirious. While it was accepted that she suffered from milk fever, this was deemed not sufficient to make her lose her mind, and then there was the question of her premeditation. Despite the anguish she clearly exhibited, the jury returned a guilty verdict; Mary was sanguine and took the news with dignity, curtseying before the court before being taken down. She was hanged on the Knavesmire and her body given over for dissection. Her seducer, of course, bore none of the consequences of his actions.

When Elizabeth Gaskell tackled the thorny issue of the seduction of working girls by rich men in *Ruth*, she incurred much enmity, even amongst friends.

Michael Simpson 1801

Thomas Hodgson of Theakston Grange, Bedale was not a well-liked man; he had been described as 'rash and resolute' – an example of his intemperate behaviour being the time when he took an axe to and killed a neighbour's horse when it wandered onto his land – the neighbour in question was Michael Simpson. Simpson called at the Grange one day on the pretext that he was concerned about Hodgson's cattle which were apparently straying. Mr. Hodgson was ill so it was Mrs. Hodgson who followed Simpson into the fields: he gave her the slip and returned to the house where he pocketed £100 from under the mattress of the Hodgson's bed, leaving Mrs. Hodgson to discover that the cattle had been deliberately herded into a ditch. Simpson returned to the Grange some days later, announcing that he had met a 'wise man' who had given him two pills: if Mr. Hodgson were to take these that night on an empty stomach then the identity of the thief would be revealed and the lost money returned. Greed obviously got the better of the gullible Mr. Hodgson's common sense and he swallowed the pills; it was not long before he 'vomited much' and died. Simpson was hanged at York's Tyburn on the Knavesmire.

Mary Chapel 1802

When Mary Chapel and her boyfriend had sex at a local feast at Ackland, she fell pregnant; her boyfriend took the King's shilling and left for the wars soon after. Mary was in the service of a Colonel Surtees at the time. She assiduously concealed the pregnancy but there comes a time when concealment becomes impossible. Mary's labour was extraordinarily painful; the baby girl was born, but found to be covered in bleeding lacerations, her mouth torn and her jawbone forced out of position. The baby was hidden between the bloody bed and the mattress of an adjoining bed.

Mary was found guilty at York Assizes but maintained that she had no knowledge of the death and had loved her baby even before it was born. She clearly acted in a fit of delirium brought on by the traumatic labour. Nevertheless, she was found guilty and sentenced to hang on the Knavesmire. Agonisingly for Mary, the execution was delayed because of a problem with the knotting of the rope. The usually festive crowd was noticeably subdued and 'Mary died without a struggle amid the audible sobs of the multitude'.

No weapon was involved in the murder so, horrible as it sounds, the injuries were inflicted by Mary with her own hands, or…the injuries were sustained in the course of the traumatic labour, or…they were inflicted accidentally by a third party anxious to help Mary in her pain.

John Terry and Joe Heald 1803

When two of 67 year old Elizabeth Smith's cows died her small dairy business was in trouble. Nevertheless, her son was able to bail her out and she continued to sell her milk from her house in Flaminshaw, Wakefield.

Terry and Heald conspired to rob Elizabeth, aware that there was a substantial amount of her son's cash in the house. But everything went wrong when the robbers were unexpectedly confronted by Elizabeth: they kicked and battered her and Terry finally cut her throat with a razor. It was only on the gallows that the whole story apparently came out: Terry jumped up and down inciting the crowd and insisted that he had killed the old lady and they were hanging an innocent man in hanging Heald. Both hanged.

Benjamin Oldroyd 1803

Forty-six year old Benjamin Oldroyd was a man of 'very weak intellect' who hanged his father. He and his mother made a feeble attempt to masquerade this as a suicide, dragging the body into the garden and attempting to suspend it from a cherry tree – a tree that was too small to hold the weight of the body. At his hanging in York, a desperate and struggling Oldroyd had to be manhandled to the noose by warders. Mrs. Oldroyd seems to have escaped any charges.

Ann Heywood 1804

Ann Heywood, a girl of little education and a big temper, was another example of the impressionable girl in service, seduced and then deserted. Bad as her situation was anyway, Heywood found herself pregnant in April 1804. She moved to Rotherham to work for the Roodhouse family, all the while concealing her pregnancy until she was full term and went into labour. The baby was duly delivered in an outhouse with other staff covering for her. Heywood went straight back to work – with blood on her clothes; the mistress of the house was naturally suspicious and sent her away to Mosborough. In fact, Ann Heywood had stabbed her newborn girl repeatedly and hid the body in the outhouse. The body was found and enquiries were made; she denied all knowledge of her actions, such was her distressed state at the time. Nevertheless, Ann Heywood was charged with murder and faced the court at York Assizes where she pleaded not guilty. Ann was obviously not well around the time of the birth, but a bloody penknife was found under her bed two days before the discovery of the baby. Disturbingly, her little girl had been slashed in the face with a wounding extending from ear to stomach: she had been disemboweled; the collar bone and ribs had been cut through. An examination showed that Heywood had in fact given birth recently and her breasts were 'full and inflamed'. She continued to deny the murder, explaining the knife by saying that she had used it on a bird. When a guilty verdict was delivered she fell to the ground 'with hysterical sobs'. While waiting to be hanged Ann Heywood confessed, and asked for the father to come to her. He did not.

John Stables 1805

When William Stables was murdered in his bed one night in Horsforth, Leeds, it would not take that much to conclude that his brother John needed to be eliminated as the prime suspect. As a result of William's death John was heir to the family estate, an inheritance that netted him £170 per year. As it happened, he saved the police a job when he hanged himself in his barn. He had clearly been depressed since his brother's murder, so much so that the inquest declared him to be a lunatic. To this day, no one has hanged for the murder of William Stables, or have they?

John Robinson 1807

John Robinson, married with four children, farmed at Mickleby near Whitby in the Esk Valley. He had a servant girl, Susannah Wilson who left his employ to go and work at Guisborough. This was a bad move for Susannah, in more ways than one. When Robinson learnt that she was very unhappy in her new job he offered to help, and arranged to meet her with the gift of a bushel of wheat, having told his family that he was going to Staithes, thus ensuring what he believed to be a good alibi. Sarah had had a premonition about the rendezvous and told friends that 'a fear had come that morning, and that if anything but good came to her they were to look to nobody but Robinson'.

During the meeting, Robinson attacked Susannah from behind with an axe: he smashed her head open and then proceeded to mutilate her body with the weapon. The problem, as Robinson saw it, was that he had made her pregnant some time earlier. Her murder was the obvious simple solution to this problem. Once the crime was committed he went on to Staithes where he spent the night. It was some five weeks before her concealed body was found, on Robinson's land. He confessed and was hanged at York, leaving a widow and his four children; his only legacy being the farm and his body for medical dissection.

Mary Bateman 1809

Forty-one year old Mary Bateman, "The Yorkshire Witch", was executed at York on March the 20th, 1809. She had been convicted of poisoning Rebecca Perigo. Mary was a farmer's daughter from Aisenby near Thirsk; she had a life-long history of criminal activity stretching back to petty theft in her childhood and latterly took to conning people with her self-proclaimed supernatural powers and healing abilities. She married and had four children and soon became a notorious fortune teller at her home in Marsh Lane in Leeds – but her biggest claim to fame was the 'Prophet Hen of Leeds' scam in 1806. People were led to believe that the end of the world had arrived when a hen began laying eggs with "Christ is coming" written on each one, neatly solving the old chicken and egg conundrum. Mary Bateman had written on the eggs using acid, and reinserted them into the hen's oviduct.

Rumour had it that Mary poisoned three people in 1803 although she was never tried or convicted. Her victims were two Quaker sisters and their mother who lived above their draper's shop in St. Peter's Square, Quarry Hill, Leeds. Mary sold them poison potions masquerading as medicines; having killed them she robbed the house and shop telling neighbours that the three women had died from plague. There was little suspicion surrounding the cause of death and no inquest.

Duplicitous as ever, Mary frequently called on the services of a "Mrs. Moore" to assist her in her scams. This fictitious lady was the source of all Mary's "wisdom" and was always consulted on behalf of Mary's clients who were led to believe their payments went to Mrs. Moore. In 1806 Mary enlisted a new alter ego called "Mrs. Blythe".

In 1806, a vulnerable, childless, middle-aged and reasonably well off couple, William and Rebecca Perigo, from Bramley approached Mary seeking her help. The Perigos were not helped by their doctor, Dr. Curzley, who concluded that the fluttering Rebecca experienced in her chest – probably atrial fibrillation – and her associated psychological issues, where she claimed hauntings by a black dog and other spirits, indicated that she was under a spell and that he could do no more for her. Mary saw this as an opportunity: she would swindle the Perigos of their money before killing them. A meeting was fixed outside, ironically, the Black Dog pub at which Mary requested an item of Rebecca's underclothing to send to Mrs. Blythe in Scarborough – a flannel petticoat was duly 'sent off'. Mrs. Blythe responded helpfully: money changed hands and horseshoes were nailed to the Perigos' front door; instructions were given to sew purses supposedly containing guinea notes and gold coins into Rebecca's bedspread and to send Mrs. Blythe a cheese followed by china and silverware and some tea and sugar. A bed and bed clothes were next because Mrs. Blythe could not sleep in her own bed due to the nocturnal battles she was having with Rebecca's demons.

Mary then delivered her coup de grâce, instructing Rebecca to bring her half a pound of honey which she would mix into some of Mrs. Blythe's special medicine. In addition, the Perigos were to eat puddings for six days into each of which they were to mix a powder that Mary would give them. All correspondence and left over pudding was to be destroyed and, if it made them ill, no doctor was to be called as Mary's treatment went beyond conventional medicine. Rebecca regularly ate her pudding but William rarely did: consequently Rebecca died in May 1806 and although William reported to a doctor that he thought poison was invloved in Rebecca's death, no post mortem was ever carried out. William Perigo continued to pay Mary for another two years until he became suspicious and checked out the purses sewn into the bedclothes: the guinea notes and gold turned out to be cabbage leaves and copper; he went to the police, who arrested Mary at an entrapment meeting to which Mary brought a bottle of arsenic and oatmeal, intended to silence William for good .

Bateman protested her innocence but poison and personal belongings of her victims, including the Perigo couple, were found at her house. She was committed for trial at the Yorkshire Lent Assizes of 1809 which opened at York Castle on 17th March before judge Sir Simon Le Blanc. Mrs. Blythe was nowhere to be found, and forensic evidence offered by a Mr. Chorley found that the remains of the honey contained highly toxic mercuric chloride.

Mary attempted to avoid execution by 'pleading her belly' – claiming that she was pregnant, but this was easily and swiftly disproved. Bateman was found guilty of fraud and murder and sentenced to death by hanging, and to be dissected the following day. She continued to deny the murder and was finally hanged alongside two men on 20th March 1809, dying 'with a lie on her lips'. The hangman was William 'Mutton' Curry. After execution, her body was put on public display: thousands paid 3d to gawp at the corpse with proceeds (£30) going to charity. Some superstitious people believed that she might be saved from death by some divine intervention at the last minute. There was also a healthy trade in strips of her skin which were sold as charms to ward off evil. After medical school dissection at Leeds Royal Infirmary, Bateman's skeleton was used in anatomy classes and later, along with a plaster cast death mask of her skull, put on display at the Thackray Museum in Leeds until 2015, when it was returned to Leeds University Medical School.

William Horsfall and the Luddite Executions 1813

The Luddites campaign of violence began in 1812; they were incensed by the introduction of new machinery, especially the shear frame, which was making skilled workers, the croppers, redundant. Their concerns matched those of large sections of the poor in general who were restless about the prolonged wars with France and an economic crisis which was putting people out of work and raising food prices. By the summer of 1812, Huddersfield, for example, was an armed camp. By 26th June almost 400 soldiers were stationed there, billeted in public houses; it is suggested that there were more British troops in Yorkshire then than Wellington had in Spain.

The White Horse was a haunt of the Luddites when, in 1812, the violence began in West Yorkshire textile districts around Huddersfield; this included the usual machine smashing and attacks on property; on 28th April 1812, however, the murder of William Horsfall, a local wool textile manufacturer and a leading advocate of the new machinery, added a more sinister element to the Luddite activism. Horsfall was shot after leaving the Warren House public house. The seven musket balls in his body ensured a slow two day death as he bled his life away.

Following an attempt to destroy Cartwright's textile mill at Rawfold near Brighouse in April 1812, over 100 Luddites had been rounded up. Sixty four were charged with a variety of offences and came before a special judicial commission at York Castle at the beginning of January 1813. Twenty four of them were convicted and seventeen sentenced to hang. The remainder were given transportation. The first of the Luddite executions was carried out on Friday, the 8th of January when three men suffered for the murder of mill owner, William Horsfall, including the Luddite's leader in Yorkshire, George Mellor. Just over a week later, on the 16th of January, the other fourteen condemned Luddites were executed for their parts in the raid on Cartwright's mill in what was to be York's biggest ever hanging event. Five of them were condemned for riot, six for burglary and three for robbery, having been convicted under the Frame Breaking Act that came into force the previous year. They were put to death in two groups by John Curry – seven at 11.00 a.m. and seven at 1.30 p.m. A "vast concourse" of people assembled on St. George's Field to see this mass "launch into eternity" as hangings were then known. Other Luddite executions took place in Lancashire.

The Hawden Hall Murder 1817

Samuel Sutcliffe was an 80 year old bachelor tailor when he was murdered at his home in Hebden Bridge by Mike Pickles and John Greenwood. What was initially intended as a robbery turned into a murder when Samuel Sutcliffe woke and disturbed the two burglars. He died for his troubles. Amongst other things, they stole a cash box containing Sutcliffe's life savings, among which were some Bank of England notes, one of which was unsigned. It was this that helped to convict Pickles and Greenwood who both hanged.

William King 1817

When a neighbour who saw William King, an edge-tool maker, prowling round his Sheffield house with a poker in his hand and asked him how he was, the toolmaker replied 'I am but poorly'. In actual fact he was in a drunken rage because his partner Sarah Tripper's soldier husband had just returned home to Sheffield. King's reaction to this was to smash her skull in with the poker at about 6.30 am as she lay in bed with her baby – the aftermath to which was witnessed by John Goodlad, a scissorsmith and a neighbour, who had forced entry into King's house when he heard screaming and saw blood on the window. Goodlad was confronted by the poker-wielding King and rushed next door to get their poker after which a frenzied poker fight ensued. Goodlad won the day; King confessed to Goodlad and although Sarah was still alive at this point she died soon after. King hanged at York.

John James 1816

The flagrant abuse of official power lies at the heart of the murder of William Ridley, a sheriff's officer of Middleham, by John James in the village of West Witton. In 1813 James was 'an involved man', meaning that he was in financial straits. Ridley was malicious and disputatious and he showed this in 1816 when he sold off James' assets at short notice. Ridley was the buyer.

When Ridley turned up at the James farm to impound hay and corn James pounced and fatally stabbed the official. James had promised Ridley that he would defend his property with his life. As it happened, the warrant of distress which Ridley had served was a fake and illegal: James was not in arrears; Ridley had malevolently concocted the whole thing – and died for his trouble. As did James, who hanged at York.

Ann Barber 1821

'A wretched victim of impure desires' is how Ann Barber was described in the local press; thirty years earlier and she would have burned at the stake for petit treason. Here in 1821 she found herself charged with both murder *and* treason – so keen were the authorities to convict her. Ann was married to James Barber and lived with him in Rothwell; she had a child from a previous marriage and two with James: Hannah and Jane. Ann was a Ranter, a non-conformist sect vilified by the established church.

After sixteen years of marriage and the two children, fifteen and nine, Ann was having an affair with their lodger, a William Thompson from Halifax. They eloped early one morning with some furniture on a handcart and took a cottage in Headingly, telling the landlord they were married; when he found out they were not married, he evicted them. Back they went to Rothwell and an amazingly forgiving James Barber allowed them to live in his marital home. The neighbours were less welcoming, however, and their disgust at the set-up forced Thompson to move out.

One day, Ann Barber roasted an apple for her husband, and warmed some beer, sweetened with sugar. Next morning he was dead; she had told a neighbour that there was no point calling a doctor as he would 'surely be dead before morning'. The inquest was held in the Barber's house with two doctors in attendance; the blackened state of Barber's lungs gave the game away: he had died from arsenic poisoning. Ann Barber's mother, Jane Smirthwaite, called in a woman, Sarah Parker, to lay out the body; she confirmed that James's ears were black and a noxious substance was dribbling from his mouth. Just before the poisoning there had been trouble in the street: Barber had fallen from a cart, Thompson had been pilloried with 'rough music' from the neighbours for taking another man's wife and Barber himself had been taunted as a cuckold.

It emerged that Ann Barber had bought some white mercury (arsenic) in Wakefield on the day of the poisoning and later poured it into that warmed beer and over the roast apple. She was arrested; at the trial at York Assizes the jury was given an option to convict her of murder, or of petit treason: they convicted on both and Barber hanged at York Castle. Thompson was never investigated, or called to give evidence.

James Mosley 1822

Over the years there have been many absurdly trivial reasons given for murdering someone. The case of James Mosley's stolen cake must rank as one of the most trivial. Sitting in The Harrow pub in Sheffield one day with a friend, Mosley's cake was taken by another drinker by the name of Beuley; predictably, a fight ensued but that was not the end of the matter. Mosley found a knife and lay in wait outside for Beuley: when he emerged with his friends, Mosley lashed out with the knife, missed and stabbed John Mackay instead. Mackay later died in Sheffield Infirmary. As it happened, Mackay had a heart condition and it was argued that he may well have died from a heart attack brought on by the shock of the injury. Nevertheless, Mosley was convicted of premeditated murder and was hanged. All over a cake.

Robert Peat 1822

A changed will in 1815 was the cause of the murder by poisoning of an old lady in Ravensworth near Richmond. Robert Peat was put out, to say the least, when his half cousin, also Robert Peat, altered his will, removing his namesake from the list of beneficiaries to the advantage of his wife. Peat was a regular visitor to his half cousin's – despite the fact that he was less than welcome – and one June day in 1922 told a neighbour he was going there because of the woman 'who wanted to wrong him out of the brass he had' and that he had a bottle of laudanum which 'would do her a trick'. When he got to the house in Ravensworth he surreptitiously added the laudanum to a leg of lamb that was simmering on the stove, concealing the consequences of his actions by suggesting there was bad water about which was making people ill. Peat had bought the laudanum from John Smith's chemist in Darlington allegedly for 'some ladies in Middleton'.

Neighbours too were given some of the stew and remarked on its strange taste and colour; in due course they and Peat's half cousin and wife were violently ill, particularly the wife. One neighbour, Mary Bolam told Peat to call a doctor for her but he demurred. She died later that night. Suspicions were raised and Peat was arrested and hanged at Durham.

Abraham Bairstan 1829

Silence is golden, or at least it was for 60 year old Bradford man Abraham Bairstan when standing in the dock accused of the murder of his wife, Sarah. Bairstan quite simply remained silent throughout the trial; prosecution questions were met with vacant stares while a witness declared that he hadn't heard Bairstan utter a word in ten years. Whether it was a neurological or psychological problem or just an impressive performance we will never know. In the event the judge put it down to 'God's will' that Bairstan was struck mute 'by the visitation and providence of God'. He was sentenced to life in an asylum and escaped the noose.

Martin Slack 1829

Probably one of the most repellent of all cases of infanticide. Poisons in the 19th century were much more easily obtainable than they are today, and many could be found in the home for perfectly good, if ill-advised, reasons. The problem, of course, was that they were sometimes used for purposes other than for which they were intended, or as listed on the tin. Arsenic and aqua fortis (nitric acid) are two examples.

Slack and his girlfriend, Elizabeth Haigh, had an illegitimate child 'on the parish' and he had spent time in Wakefield House of Correction for defaulting on the idemnity to provide for her. On release he was obliged to pay maintenance but this all contributed to his feeling of resentment against the child and which manifested itself in the atrocity of that morning. On a previous occasion he had rejected the baby saying he wanted no such thing near him.

Seventeen year old Martin Slack visited his five week old baby daughter on November 23rd 1829; she lived with her mother in her parents' house in West Bar, Sheffield. When left alone with her, Slack poured nitric acid down her throat. Symptoms caused by ingestion include acute pain in the throat, vomiting of a bloody fluid, cold sweats and convulsions. What that baby went through is unimaginable.

When Elizabeth saw what had happened, 'smoke' was coming from its mouth and it was dribbling a liquid the colour of brimstone, some of which ran on to her arm and burnt it. She screamed for help for her baby but when doctors arrived, they were unable to neutralize the acid which was by now in the digestive tract. The warm water, magnesia and carbonate of potash were to no avail. The baby died and Slack was arrested. He was hanged at York, protesting his innocence to the end. His corpse was taken to Sheffield for dissection.

The Bill O'Jacks Murder 1832

The Bill O'Jacks pub on Marsden Moor above Huddersfield was the setting for a grisly, as yet unsolved, murder. On April 2nd 1832 a landlord and his gamekeeper son, 46 year old Thomas and 84 year old William Bradbury, were violently murdered at The Bill O' Jacks or The Moorcock, reported at the time as 'one of the most diabolical murders ever committed' in 'a scene of bloody carnage that sent shockwaves through the local community and beyond'. According to witness accounts at the inquest, blood covered the 'floor, furniture, walls and stairs of the pub as if there had been a violent struggle'. 'The walls and flags streaming with gore' according to one colourful contemporary newspaper report. The pub was demolished in 1937 but not before it had satisfied the morbid voyeurism of thousands of tourists.

Ursula Lofthouse 1835

Ursula Lofthouse hanged for poisoning her husband with arsenic. Despite the fact that she was the last woman to be publicly hanged in Yorkshire and 2,000 people came to gloat and gawp, the woman is more famous for the fact that she was hanged in a triple hanging by the serially drunk and seriously incompetent Mutton Curry at York Castle.

Charles Batty 1836

The case of Charles Batty was unusual because he was sentenced to hang at York – not for murder, but for attempted murder. Batty and his common-law wife, Elizabeth, were living lives of penury; he had just been discharged from the army and settled in Sheffield, jobless with no money coming in. Things came to a terrible head with only one potato in the house and Elizabeth taking refuge in her bed from hunger and from Batty. Batty demanded Elizabeth do something about the food situation; she complained and Batty grabbed her by the throat, slashed her throat with a razor, threw her over the banister and left her in the street moaning that she had pawned his clothes and that he should have 'finished' her long ago.

Amazingly, Elizabeth survived her injuries but, as far as the judge was concerned she was left for dead by Batty, so Batty hanged.

Thomas Williams 1837

There is little doubt that basket maker Thomas Williams' brain was addled by the copious amounts of alcohol he routinely consumed. There is less doubt that drink was the cause of Williams' dismissal from George Moore of Silver Street Head, Sheffield and that it compelled him to seek revenge. Williams, 29, indiscreetly told a man called William Buggins in the Black Swan about this desire for vengeance and, sure enough, one day walked into his old firm and smashed his replacement, Froggat, on the skull with a bill hook, or hedging bill. The hook penetrated Froggat's brain an inch deep and Williams struggled to get it out again; he died soon after. Williams left the murder scene for a pub, Lindley's Public House, where he announced to the world what he had done: 'I have killed old Frog'. When arrested, Williams admitted that he would be glad if Frogatt died because he was a 'damned rascal and wanted to take the bread off my trencher'. His death would be good for the George Moore business; if he was not dead yet he would go back and finish him.

At the trial in York, a plea of insanity was rejected and Williams was sentenced to death. Frogatt was not the only victim of Williams' intemperance: the murderer left a widow and five children who presumably found themselves in the workhouse. This was Williams's penitent and evangelical speech from the scaffold: ' Fellow-men, you are come to witness a spectacle of intemperance – an awful scene: I hope this will make a lasting impression upon every soul before me. A man in the prime of life, 30 years of age, cut off through this diabolical crime of intemperance. Is there a drunkard before me? Yea, I see many. Let him go home, and be so no more. Is there a liar? Let him speak truth for the future, and turn to God with full purpose of heart. I have to inform you that I am leaving a grateful partner behind me; one that is walking in the commandments of the Lord, and one that delights in her God'.

Frank Parker 1837

Frank Parker's was an unusual and sad case. He was confined to York Lunatic Asylum but demanded he be released and imprisoned at the Castle instead. Despite having his arms pinned to his sides to prevent him harming himself Parker still succeeded in kicking a fellow lunatic to death because he believed that he had been planted there to kill him. At his trial Parker said he simply 'got in first'. He was convicted of murder and got his wish, spending the rest of his life in a cell in York Castle.

Alexander MacLaghlin Smith 1840

When PC William Duke reported for his shift in April 1840 he could have had no idea what awaited him. Duke was called to an incident in Huddersfield where an angry gardener, Smith, was exhibiting violent and abusive behaviour over a transaction relating to some plants. He tried to stab Duke with a pruning knife when approached; astonishingly this weapon remained in his possession. Duke clapped him in irons in a cell but Smith broke free and stabbed Duke; two other policemen struck him with their truncheons but he escaped and went and sat in the George pub, blood on his clothes. Duke died of his wounds. Smith was declared insane at his trial at York and was detained for her Majesty's Pleasure. PC Dawson also received life-threatening gashes.

James Bardsley 1840

Some murders are suddenly and swiftly committed. Such was the case with wayward James Bardsley when at Lees on Saddleworth Moor he slew his father, John Bardsley, in a fit of supreme temper. John Bardsley was quietly reading his bible with his daughter and her friend when James came home and started eating some bread and cheese; John rebuked him for this and received knife wounds to his face and body from James by way of response. His sister fled the house and called for help. When she and some neighbours returned, James was calmly eating and drinking and covered in his father's blood. James Bardsley was later hanged in York.

John Burlinson, Henry Nuttall and Charles Gill 1841

The White Hart, a small pub in Knaresborough market place, was a bad place. In 1841 Joseph Cocker was landlord there, a widower who lived alone. One night in June three Knaresborough men called in for a drink: the intention of John Burlinson was to rob the pub, with a little help from his friends, Henry Nuttall and Charles Gill. When Cocker refused to serve them – they had already consumed five pints – Burlinson hit him on the head with a hammer; the landlord pleaded with them 'not to murder him'. The robbers suggested concealing Cocker down in the cellar – all of this was witnessed by a Mrs. Snow, a daring lady from next door who had heard the commotion and went to look through the window. Gill struck Cocker four or five more times with the hammer. After robbing Cocker, the men fled down Jockey Lane (the Synagogues) onto the High Street to High Bridge from where the hammer was despatched into the River Nidd. Meanwhile Mr. Snow collected his pistol and summoned David Vickerman, a policeman. In the pub they found a blood-soaked Cocker with a poker lying next to him and the walls blood-spattered. Thomas Beaumont, the surgeon, was called but could not save him. All three robbers – murderers now – were arrested later that night and relieved of their blood-soaked clothing which was later used as evidence. All three were sentenced to death by hanging at York.

John Rodda 1846

John Rodda must go down as one of the most repugnant and sinister of Yorkshire's murderers: he callously killed his eighteen month old daughter, Mary, by pouring oil of vitriol, sulphuric acid, down her throat so that he could claim the £2.10s burial fee from his burial club, or dead club as they were sometimes known. He was sentenced to hang at York at which 'a convulsive struggle ensued – and the mortal ceased to exist'.

Mirfield Murder House 1847

A stolen tea caddy seems to have been the catalyst for a scene of carnage like no other. Caroline Ellis was the servant girl of the Wraith family who lived at the secluded Water Royd House. Her marriage had been arranged for Sunday 16th May 1847, the day after her funeral. Caroline Ellis had argued with Patrick Reid, a knife and razor grinder, over the theft of a tea caddy. James Wraith ordered him not to darken his door again. Reid shouted, "I'll revenge on you either at one time or another". He then left and called on Thomas Kilty, an Irish hawker, for a soldering iron.

The dreadful events of May 12th 1847 went as follows: at 12.35 pm Reid returned to Water Royd and spoke with Caroline Ellis for about five minutes. He took the soldering iron from a basket and struck the girl on the head. She screamed and staggered to the back door but Reid struck her again and she fell to the ground; her skull was smashed and her teeth knocked out. Hearing the commotion, Mr

Wraith came out of the dining room, and, still carrying his silver pint tankard full of beer, went into the passage; Reid delivered such a blow to Wraith's head that the iron detached itself from the handle. Mr. Wraith staggered back into the dining room while Reid dashed into the kitchen to get the poker, just in time to meet Mrs. Wraith running out of the dining room for the front door. He struck her two or three times on the head; one of her eyes was knocked out; he then went through the pockets of the bleeding and unconscious James Wraith. There was a knock on the kitchen door.

Reid stole some money out of the drawers, Mr. Wraith's watch from Mr. Wraith, and the ring from Mrs. Wraith's finger. There was another knock on the kitchen door; Reid opened it cautiously to find a hawker, Michael McCabe, on the doorstep who asked Reid if there was anything he needed. Reid replied, "No sir"; he shut and bolted the door and resumed ransacking the drawers in the house where he found a packet containing two razors.

He took one out and cut the throats of all three victims, washed his hands and wiped them on the towel and left the house by the kitchen door which he locked behind him, throwing both the key and the soldering iron into the well in the garden, then hurried home. It was not very long before local people heard of the atrocity and invaded the house, trampling all over the evidence and morbidly looting items from the crime scene as souvenirs.

Patrick Reid and Michael McCabe were taken into custody on suspicion of involvement in the murders, and committed to York Assizes, charged with the wilful murder of James Wraith only. McCabe turned Queen's evidence, so only Reid was brought to trial. The trial was a fiasco: confused by contradictory evidence, confused about the omission of the other two murders from the charge, confused by who had done what, the jury could not agree and Reid was initially found not guilty. However, on 20th December Reid and McCabe were sentenced to hang at York. Then, immediately after passing sentence the judge was informed that Reid had made a full confession, exonerating McCabe completely. Reid's defence counsel, who had been trying to lay all the blame on McCabe, had had Reid's written confession in his pocket all through the trial. McCabe was reprieved, and ordered to be transported for life. The judge was of the belief that McCabe was involved in the murders "to some extent", although there was no evidence to support that belief. McCabe came back from Australia to live in Huddersfield, where he died around 1880.

This the report of Reid's execution as reported in *The Leeds Mercury*: 'Probably on no occasion has an execution, within our recollection, drawn together so vast a concourse of spectators. Besides bringing together a very large proportion of the inhabitants of York and its more immediate vicinity, many towns in the West Yorkshire Riding added their thousands to swell the general throng From Halifax, Bradford, Wakefield, Barnsley, Leeds, Huddersfield, Dewsbury, Mirfield, Pontefract, and indeed from every other place… some idea of the proportion which Leeds bore, may be formed from the fact that by the 7.20 a.m. train alone there were conveyed to York more than 1,000 extra passengers. All the available carriages were put into use, and still hundreds were left behind, at that time, to be conveyed by a subsequent train. This, however, gives but a very imperfect estimate of the number of persons that went from Leeds to York, as it is exclusive to pedestrians, many of whom even as early as the previous night, left this little town to visit the scene of the execution. It may be truly said of this occasion, that the soul-depressing exhibition of a criminal on the scaffold, drew more persons early from their rest on the coldest morning of the winter, than the most transcendent exhibition of virtue could probably have by a accomplished with all the charms and temptations of one of summer's most attractive days. The crowds expected Reid to make some remarks from the scaffold but this did not happen thus disappointing the spectators. However, just before the bolt was drawn, he said to the officers around him, ''I wish to say that I alone am the guilty person, that McCabe is entirely innocent, that no human being in the world had anything to do with it but myself." Scarcely had a moment elapsed after the drop fell, before one or two boys who witnessed it were in the hands of the police for pocket-picking'. The report fails to mention that the execution was bungled by the hangman and Reid suffered a slow and agonising death.

The funerals evoked just as much morbid ghoulishness: the day before, the three corpses were laid out in the drawing room and seen by hundreds of people. Mr. and Mrs. Wraith were buried in Mirfield Churchyard before a huge crowd; a similar throng witnessed Caroline Ellis being laid to rest in the burial ground of the Wesleyan Chapel. Afterwards, the crowd made its way to Water Royd. Similar scenes were repeated on Sunday and Monday; the number of sightseers was so great on the Sabbath that policemen had to be stationed in the different rooms to preserve some dignity and hurry the visitors through so others could take their places. After the funeral, the floors of the rooms were scrubbed clean leaving only a few spots of blood on the walls and ceiling of the dining room.

However, flowers, part of the hedge and leaves were taken from the garden as mementoes. The house remained a tourist attraction and 'persons in holiday attire and vehicles from all parts continued to disturb the peace of Mirfield… the interior inspection was discontinued after May 29th but still the crowds gathered to gaze at the house'.

The Spectator of 19th February 1848 reported: 'On the day of the execution of Patrick Reid for the murders at Mirfield, Andrew Purchase, a showman, bought Reid's clothes and the rope with which he was hanged. He procured a full length wax figure and likeness of Reid, dressed it in his clothes, and placed the hanging-noose in the hands of the figure. This exhibition he opened to the public at a low admission-price in Leeds. Such crowds flocked to the sight that free passage of the streets was hindered. A few days since the stream of visitors slackened, on a rumour that the things shown were not genuine! On this check, the showman hired Nathaniel Howard, the hangman, and brought him express from York to attend his show in person, and display the mode of managing his professional duty. Howard vouches to each new audience for the genuineness of Reid's garments; and by experiments with the waxen figure shows the causes why the noose was partially ineffectual at the execution: each time he attributes the slipping of the rope to the prisoner's curiosity in turning round, and to the rope's having been frozen stiff!' The sickening voyeurism continued; at the Bradford Fair *The Leeds Mercury* reported on 12th June 1847: 'The fair has been, on account of the fine weather, thronged. The shows and sights are unusually meagre and uninteresting. No less than three puppet shows were in the market, having in large letters announced a view of the Mirfield murders, for the gratification of the morbid curiosity of the ignorant'.

Sarah and Abigail Stubbs 1848

The Commercial Inn, Harrogate, was the setting for a murder inquest in 1848. Two daughters, Sarah and Abigail Stubbs, had thrown their father down the stairs to his death – they were indignant and unhappy about the pittance they got from their mother, Ann Stubbs, for the help they had given her with the washing she had taken in at their home in Tower Street. The girls were later acquitted.

George Howe 1849

George Howe was a railway labourer in Yarm; he murdered his baby daughter with oxalic acid in January 1849; the baby's mother – his second wife – died in childbirth in October 1848. He had been restrained from harming the infant on previous occasions. Kidney failure is the usual cause of death.

William Green 1850

James Smith was the keeper at the Hebden Bridge toll house. He was found with his throat cut; the locals had meticulously cleaned up the mess before any evidence could be gleaned from the scene. The only positive clue left was that two people had obviously slept in the bed, but this was denied by the local vicar, an irritating amateur dectective, who insisted that Smith slept alone – on both sides of the bed. A suspect was Enoch Heliwell who lived over in Burnley and enjoyed a fractious relationship with Smith – Heliwell, however, had a sound alibi. This left William Green as the last person to be seen with Smith; Green confessed and bloodstained clothes were found in his house, but he later retracted his confession. His indecision was corroborated by witnesses who confirmed that Green was not wearing those clothes that night. Meanwhile, a clasp knife was found.

The police were clutching at straws and suggested that Heliwell may have hired Green to do the murder. Green was arrested but released on £1,000 bail; Green subsequently put on a dramatic performance in the dock which won him some sympathy. A letter was received confirming that Green was indeed the murderer but the author was later found to be insane. The case remains unsolved.

James Doyle and Ann Smith 1850

Wakefield Railway Station was the setting for a truly shocking case of infanticide. The body of a child 'with its throat cut from ear to ear', according to the *Household Narrative*, was found in a 'common blue box tied round with cord'. It was deduced that the killers had to be on a train that had just departed Wakefield for Thornhill; Doyle and Smith were arrested and charged at York where they both received life sentences.

Alfred Waddington 1852

The Times of August 20th 1852 reported the shocking murder of Elizabeth Slater in Sheffield: 'An illegitimate child, nearly two years old, has had its head cut off by its father, who also attempted to murder its mother and another young woman. The murderer's name is Alfred Waddington, a grinder, residing in Lord-street, Park… The murdered child was called Elizabeth Slater, the daughter of Sarah Slater, of Brown-street, Park, and was about a year and nine months old. On Monday the mother took out a summons, which was to have been heard today, against Waddington, for neglecting to maintain the child. He saw her in the street on Wednesday, and swore he would never pay another farthing towards the support of the child. On Wednesday evening the mother left her child in the care of a little girl called Barlow, and then went to attend the females' evening class at the Mechanics' Institution. About half-past 8 o'clock Waddington appeared at the door of the classroom and called out "Sarah Slater, you're wanted." She went to him, and asked "What have you done with the child?" She told him, and he then said, "You must go with me; it has fallen off a wall and has broken its neck." She immediately ran out of the room with him. On arriving in Silvester-lane he said she need not trouble herself for he had murdered the child. He pulled out a large clasp knife and said "Here's some of its blood." The monster then fiercely attacked her and attempted to cut her throat. She guarded her neck with her hands, which were shockingly lacerated, and a little boy who saw the struggle called out "Murder!" Waddington then ran up Earle-street, and the poor woman was taken home. Waddington was shortly afterwards met by a young woman called Sarah Dobson, who resides in Duke-lane, Sheffield-moor, a companion of the young woman Slater. Having heard rumours of the murder and the attack upon Slater, the young woman asked him what he had done with her and his child. He at once attacked her with his knife, and wounded her severely about the face. Her violent screams caused him to run away. About 2 o'clock this morning, however, he gave himself up to a night watchman, and at the Town-hall he described the exact place where the murdered child might be found. He said he took it from the little girl Barlow, carried it into Cutler's-wood, Heely, near Sheffield, and there cut its head off. At daylight this morning two policemen went to the place mentioned, and there they found the body of the child. Its head was lying several feet from its body.'

The following day the inquest was held on the infant's death: the body of the murdered child was brought into the room in a basket, and viewed by the coroner and jury: 'an appalling spectacle' according to *The Times*. Waddington admitted murdering the child, but was sorry that he had done so. He said he was much attached to Sarah Slater, but she had taken up with another man, and he wished it had been Sarah rather than the child he had killed. The jury returned a verdict of "Wilful Murder", and the prisoner was committed to York Castle for trial. He was executed at York on January 8th 1853. Before his execution Waddington did show genuine remorse for his actions and spent his final hours praying in his cell. A crowd of 8,000 gathered to watch him hang.

James Barbour 1853

When Alexander Robinson set off on a four day sales trip to Sheffield for Mr. D Barbour, his Doncaster linen draper employer, and failed to return on schedule, there was little cause for concern. It was only when his body was found in a ditch in Midhill Black Bank with gunshot wounds to the head and neck that anyone started to take interest. While in Sheffield, Robinson met Barbour's cousin, something of a delinquent, unemployed and busy collecting payments owed to his uncle. However, he inveigled his way into Robinson's confidence: the pair went to the pub and later left, presumably to collect more money. Witnesses reported seeing Barbour indiscreetly flashing Robinson's silver watch which was later pawned. Barbour was later arrested, charged with Robinson's murder and taken to York where he protested that another man called McCormack was responsible. All to no avail: Barbour swung, but in an excruciating and painfully slow way when the bolt on the trap stuck.

Henry Dobson 1853

Henry Dobson had been consorting with and living with a nineteen year old prostitute, Catherine, 'Kitty', Sheridan, whom he violently abused. When she left him, the next time they passed in a Wakefield street she shunned him. Dobson made her pay for this slight by cutting her throat ear to ear. He boasted of his deed and was sentenced to hang. Unusually, the jury did not bother to retire – so unanimous and sure were they of the verdict that they returned a guilty verdict from the box. Dobson paid twice for his crime when Nathaniel Howard, the 73 year old hangman, botched the execution gifting Dobson a slow and agonising death.

Isabella Campbell and Caroline Nicholson 1853

These two 19 year old women of easy virtue were on their way back from the York Horse Fair when they came upon John Hall staggering out of the White Horse in Pavement flush with drink and with the proceeds from selling his horse at the fair. The women pounced and led him down to the King's Staith and the icy cold River Ouse en route to their lodgings. Inevitably Hall ended up in the river and the women repaired to McGregor's Dram Shop on Low Ousegate; Hall's body was found downstream near the public washing area known as Pudding Holes; the women were arrested in Nessgate. A purse was found on Isabella Campbell.

At the Guildhall magistrates the women were remanded in the House of Correction at Toft Green and later convicted of the wilful murder of John Hall.

The Great Burdon Poisoning Case 1855

The Woolers lived a comfortable life in Great Burdon near Darlington, then in the North Riding. Joseph Wooler, it seemed, showed an unhealthy interest in the health of his wife, Jane. Indeed, he went so far as to borrow an enema syringe from a surgeon friend. When Jane died, traces of arsenic were found in her rectum which naturally led to the not unreasonable suggestion that Joseph had been injecting Jane with the poison. One of three examining doctors, a Dr. Jackson, had asserted that he was unhappy with the conclusion that Jane had died from natural causes. At Durham Assizes, confusingly for the jury, these doctors were criticised for continuing to treat Jane when they suspected she might be being poisoned. The case was complicated yet further when it was revealed that both Wooler and the judge were freemasons. Verdict: not guilty.

Abraham Jessop 1855

Abraham Jessop was a drinker – a habit which did nothing for his relationship with his new wife in their home at Clayton-on-the Heights near Halifax – the magazine *Household Narrative* described the relationship as 'domestic differences'. Jessop could see no solution to the problem so he arranged to meet his wife, taking two guns with him. He shot her through the heart and then in the head with separate pistols, finally turning one of the guns on himself. Amazingly, his fatally wounded wife managed to run out the door before dying several weeks later.

William Dove 1856

William Dove, a young tenant farmer and a Methodist from Newby Wiske just north of Thirsk, was tried and executed in 1856 for poisoning his wife Harriet. The trial was complicated by the fact that Dove had been involved with Henry Harrison, a Leeds 'wizard'; he also exhibited through words and actions a strong affinity for magic and satanic powers, all of which was used in an attempt to prove Dove's insanity. Dove, it seems, murdered his wife to realise a tempting prediction made by Harrison that he would remarry a better looking and wealthy woman. Dove engaged Harrison to perform various acts of magic, and made a written pact with the devil. The Dove-Harrison relationship started soon after Dove moved to industrial, cholera-ridden Leeds with his new wife after failing as a farmer; the marriage was hardly stable and Harrison identified the couple as vulnerable sorts he could exploit. Pseudo-medicine, poisons were the stock-in-trade of such charlatans as Harrison, along with a considerable spoonful of duplicity and lies. He 'prescribed' strychnine to see off Harriet Dove. Her husband was tried at the Summer Assizes in York and hanged on St George's Field opposite the Castle.

John Hannah 1856

When John Hannah, wife murderer, was executed at York Castle 5,000 people came to gawp at the spectacle. They were not to be disappointed: Hannah was duly pinioned, he went white and trembled visibly. The hymn book he was holding in his hand fell to the floor and then he was reported 'from the convulsive motions of his body, to suffer greatly for moments'. Hannah had murdered his estranged wife, Jane Banham, in the parlour of the Malt Mill in Armley, because she refused to go back to Manchester with him.

Sarah Jemmison 1857

'In the Way from Whitby to Gisburgh, we passed by Freeburgh Hill, which they told us was cast up by the Devil, at the Entreaty of an old Witch, who desired it, that from thence she might espy her Cow in the Moor'. *Select Remains of the Learned John Ray, with his Life* by William Derham, page 177. Published 1760.

It seems that the satanic associations of Freeborough Hill lived on until well into the next century. Sarah Jemmison (or Jamieson), about 30, worked for a farmer, William Pearson, at Egton; she decided to farm out her baby son, Joseph, to a Mrs. Marley who lived in Sleights near Whitby. But the arrangement lasted only a short while: Sarah could not afford to pay Mrs. Marley so had decided to take him back and leave him in the workhouse. The baby was wearing a white shirt when she collected him. Joseph was returned to Sarah, much to the annoyance of Pearson who was reluctant to feed another mouth. Sarah and Joseph went to Moorsholm in a cart where Sarah was supposedly to leave Joseph with some friends at Mangra Park, but the baby was never seen again. That is until seven months later a dog was found chewing a human leg. A search revealed a child's white shirt, thighbone and skull which had suffered trauma which could not have been 'inflicted during life'. In fact, the baby had been decapitated with a sharp instrument.

Sarah was arrested and found guilty of infanticide, or "murder of a bastard", at York; a plea for mercy saved her life when the death sentence was commuted to penal servitude for life.

The John Sagar Affair 1857

Workhouses were repellent enough places without the staff indulging in abusive, nefarious deeds. That's exactly what John Sagar, master of the Keighley Oakworth Exley Head workhouse, did when he allegedly killed his wife by administering arsenic. But Barbara Sagar was probably not the only victim: even though infant mortality was notoriously high, the presence of the bodies of the Sagars' nine children in Haworth burial ground could not fail to raise suspicions.

Sagar, who had had one hand amputated, was tried for murder. He was revealed to be a sadist who frequently beat his wife and often locked her in the workhouse mortuary; sexual liaisons with female inmates were not unusual. Evidence from a man called Milligan, a medical officer of dubious reputation in the employ of the Keighley workhouse, found that there was no arsenic in any of the various ointments Barbara Sagar was routinely taking. This was at odds with the police surgeon's discovery of two grams of the poison in her body and the fact that she had told neighbours that her husband was poisoning her. The result was confusion. The prosecution withdrew their case: verdict not guilty. It is worth noting that when the Sagars sold their shop in Cullingworth to take up the posts at the workhouse a stomach pump was listed amongst the contents.

James Atkinson 1858

In 1858 the badly mutilated, almost decapitated, body of Mary Jane Scaife was taken to the New Inn in Darley to await the coroner. The murderer, James Atkinson, was refused permission to give his 'sweetheart' one last kiss.

Joseph Shepherd 1858

Joseph Shepherd, 22, hailed from Holdsworth near Halifax. He was described as 'a most hardened and impertinent wretch and blasphemer'. While waiting to be hanged he professed his desire for a 'good blow-out' before he died, that he would prefer to be shot than hanged and preferred hanging in summer more than winter. This was another botched hanging, this time by Thomas Askern, enjoyed by 10,000 people at York. Shepherd's crime? He shot Bethel Parkinson to death on Wadworth Moor.

John Taylor Whitworth 1858

John Taylor Whitworth was convicted at York Assizes of the murder of his girlfriend Sally Hare who died of wounds inflicted upon her by Whitworth, while walking with him on Throapham Common near Rotherham. Sally Hare, aged 18 was a servant of Mr. Cuthbert, a farmer of Laughton-en-le-Morthen, Rotherham. This is Sally's graphic statement made shortly before she died: "The prisoner and I have kept company for about three years. Last night the 30th of September, he came to see me. My mistress went to bed and left us up together in the kitchen. My master went to bed about 8 o'clock. The prisoner and I sat quietly together till about 1 o'clock, and no angry words passed between us. About 1 o'clock he left the house to start for home, and asked me to accompany him a short distance. It was a beautiful starlit night, and I consented. We left the house together and got as far as the little common. He then accused me of going with another young man, whose name he did not mention. We had some words about it, and he asked me to take poison. He said, 'If you will take some, I will take some too, and we can die together'. I said I would not. He said, 'If you don't, I will kill you'. I said, 'Though you do kill me, I won't take any'. Immediately on leaving the house, and before he accused me of infidelity, he had attempted to take improper liberties with me, and had made indecent proposals to me. I would not accede to his proposals, and he then accused me of going with another man. After I refused to take the poison he got hold of me, threw me on the ground, put his knee upon me, pulled out a knife, opened it, and cut my throat. Before he cut me I implored him not to kill me, but he put one hand on my mouth, and with the other cut my throat. I got the knife out of his hand, and managed to get up, but in the struggle I cut my hands and fingers very much. When I had got up he stabbed me in the throat with the knife, and I got hold of his hair, threw him backwards, and so managed to escape. When I was on the ground, and endeavouring to rise, he stamped upon my head with his foot two or three times. I ran home, bleeding all the way, and went straight to my mistress's bedroom. I said that Whitworth had tried to murder me. My mistress got up and endeavoured to stop the bleeding with some clothes, and I was put to bed, where I have been ever since."

It is interesting to compare Whitworth's version of the events that night: "The girl went out with me from the house, and we went together as far as we had often gone before, and then we stopped for a short time. She asked me when I was going with her to the feast at Tattershall Thorpe, and I said I thought there was no good me going there, and that she did not want me. She said if I did not care for her, she did not care for me. I said we have not been long together, but I hope to be comfortable. We got to further words, and I told her I thought she went with another man. She said before she would tell me she would lose her life. I said I did not wish to go with anyone else while she went with me. I then asked her if she would go any further, and she said she would not. She said, 'We will part as we have always done before.' She then told me to sit down and she would sit on my knee. I sat down, with my feet in the hollow of the ground, and she sat on my knee. When she sat down she said, 'What have you got here?' I said 'It's my knife.' She asked me to let her look at it, and I asked her what for. She said she thought it was as much her knife as mine, and then she got the knife out of my hand and opened it. I said she should not open it, and that I should shut it again. I tried to get it out of her hand to shut it, and she said before I should have it she would try for her life. I tried to get the knife again, and it came through her fingers. She said, 'Bill, you have cut my fingers; and I said, 'I'll have my knife if it cuts your face off.' She then said, 'Then, you shall try for it.' So I tried to get it again, and she got hold of the hair of my head. I asked her what she meant, and she said if I would not let her go she would let me know what she meant. I said we had better part good friends, and that I should have my knife. She then got hold of my hair again, and pulled me down. I rolled her twice over and her head caught my feet. I said I should not stand that, and she said she would not give into me. I told her she had better be starting, and she struck at me with the knife in her hand. I tried to keep her off my face, and it went on my jacket sleeve. I tried to get the knife again, but she had fast hold of it, and she said she would not part with it. Rolling about together, the knife went in the side of her face, and I tried to get it out of her hand. She stuck to it fast, and threw me over again. She then said, 'Oh, Bill, the knife has run into my neck.' I said, 'I cannot help it; you should have let go of the knife, and let me go.' She said, 'Let's get up, and I will give you a kiss and let you go.' So we got up, and I said, 'Come, then, my lass, put your arms round my neck and I'll give you a kiss.' Then she came to me and said, 'Oh, Bill,' I said, 'What, my lass?' She said, 'My throat's cut.' I asked her what with, and she said, 'This knife here.' She said, 'I will give you a kiss for the last.' I said, 'Come, then,' and while I put my arms round her neck she struck the knife right at my throat, and said, 'Go to hell with you, Bill.' I then fell on my back, and she ran away. When I got up I saw no one, and made the best of my way home. I was taken to the lockup, and did not know what it was for till this morning, when they told me it was for cutting the throat of Sally Hare. I was taken to see her, and gave her three kisses, and was then brought away."

Whitworth was convicted of wilful murder and hanged at York.

Charles Normington 1859

Sixty-seven year old Richard Broughton was out walking one day in 1859 from Roundhay through Seacroft to Harehills, still largely rural in those days. He was accosted by two men who relieved him of his watch and beat him savagely about the head and face. Broughton died soon after. A number of suspects were questioned but released until 19 year old Charles Normington was put in the frame and arrested in Sheffield. He was tried at York, maintaining that another man killed Broughton – but this took no account of his blood-stained shirt. On being convicted of murder, Normington finally confessed and was hanged. Such was the notoriety of the case that a number of people wanted part of it, writing to the police insisting that they were Normington's accomplices. 10,000 or so attended the execution, hushed by the spectacle of hanging one so young, apparently.

John Riley 1859

Hull man John Riley was a hardened drinker and a convicted wife-beater. His wife, Alice, was a trained seamstress but he drove her to prostitution to pay for his habit; she then turned to drink herself – to soften the blows and shame no doubt. One June day a neighbour came calling but got no answer. On looking through the window, she saw Riley hanging; when she and others broke in they cut Riley down, just alive. Alice, however, was found dead upstairs – her throat had been cut with a kitchen knife. When Riley hanged at York, he left two orphans.

The Elizabeth Mitchell Case 1860

The killing of 14 year old Elizabeth Mitchell in Wakefield remains unsolved to this day. She was left alone in Upton Farm one afternoon which she spent playing with other children. Later she was joined in the farm by a farm worker, George Thorpe. Elizabeth's body was later found in the coal house. Police were called and Thorpe was arrested and taken into custody. The case against him was strengthened when a trunk containing his blood-stained smock was discovered. The girl had been shot in the back. However, there was only circumstantial evidence to convict Thorpe and no motive – she had not been raped for example. Thorpe walked free.

William Walsh 1860

William Walsh, 48, was a very cruel man. He lived with his wife in Navigation Road, York but totally ignored her, even moving his mistress into the marital home. Mrs. Walsh was neglected, starving and pestered with vermin while William Walsh lived it up in the next room. When she was discovered, in an advanced stage of malnutrition and emaciation, she was removed to the workhouse where she died after three days. William Walsh got seven years for manslaughter.

John Dodds 1860

John Dodds was discharged after standing trial for the murder of widow Margaret Spring, proprietress of the Pennyman's Arms in North Ormesby near Middlesbrough. Margaret took in lodgers and was unfortunate enough to have let a room to John Dodds, a well-known drunk, in 1860. The relationship, however, went a lot further than just lodging and Dodds had a reputation for abusing Margaret as well as for drink. After one particularly abusive incident in November 1860 the charlady at the pub, Mary Haggerstone, watched as Margaret threw Dodds' pint onto the fire and told him to find lodgings elsewhere. Dodds reacted by punching her to the ground and repeatedly beating her about the head and face, grabbing her throat, kicking her legs and kneeling on her stomach. Another lodger came to her aid; Dodds fled vowing vengeance on the whole house. Despite Margaret being severely injured, no doctor was called until mid December when only minor injuries were found and treated; Margaret died on Christmas Eve.

Dodds was arrested and charged with murder. The post-mortem revealed bleeding on the brain which was the cause of death but no one could say for sure that Dodds had caused this. Hence his discharge.

James Waller 1861

When William Smith, gamekeeper for Timothy Horsfall at Hawksworth Hall in Bingley, irritated poacher James Waller, it seems as though revenge was inevitable. Waller let himself be seen by Smith who gave chase; Waller shot 'Davey' twice in the chest. He was found in a barn 'pale and haggard and much reduced'. The inquest was held at the Angel Inn, Baildon at which a constable reported that he heard Waller say that 'he would blow Smith's brains out'. Ann Wilkinson said that Waller came to her house and asked for a vantage point from which he could see and shoot at Smith. Waller pleaded not guilty at York Assizes but he was hung in front of a crowd of 10,000 people. His last words were that he hoped there was no bad feeling between him and Smith.

Mary Ryan's Double Infanticide 1862

Mary Ryan could take no more of the beatings and bullying inflicted on her by her evil husband, so she picked up her two children and carried them to a mill dam in Bradford's Frederick Street where all three drowned. The younger child was nine months old.

Henry Sherwin 1863

Money, of course, in whatever form, can be the root of, or the route to, evil. Sheffield bailiff John Sturdy was to discover this when he went to collect, perhaps over-zealously, £1.1s.9d arrears from Henry Sherwin in Broomhall Street. Quite a sum back then. Sherwin was out but his wife let him in and Sturdy made himself comfortable in a chair to await Sherwin's return.

When he got home with a friend to find the hated bailiff in his chair, Sherwin was none too pleased and shouted 'Bugger thy eyes, I'll kill thee'. Sherwin was true to his word: the Sherwin children fled the house, Sturdy staggered out with two black eyes and other wounds: three days later he died in the workhouse hospital. The dilemma for the coroner was whether the death was caused by the beating or in a drunken binge just before death. The doctors testified that Sturdy died from injuries to the brain, liver and kidneys. The case was sent to the assizes at York where a manslaughter verdict was returned. Sherwin got five years but was released eleven months early on a ticket of leave – a document of parole issued when a convict could demonstrate they could be trusted with freedom.

Brian Terry 1864

No one and nowhere is safe when insanity runs amok. The body of 35 year old Sarah Terry was found in a stable at Green House Farm near Keighley; she had been virtually decapitated and there was a gash from one ear to one breast. All evidence pointed to Brian Terry. Neighbours described the behaviour of her husband as 'a low and desponding state of mind'. He was found in a barn a few days later, nonchalantly stuffing bread and cheese into his mouth and repeating the words 'It's a bad job'.
It transpired that Terry was watering the cows and Sarah was giving milk to a calf; Terry complained that she had not given enough milk and came up behind her and hit her with an iron bar. She ran towards him and slit her throat with a razor. Her dying words were 'Oh Brian, the Lord save me'. Insanity ran in the Terry family, and Brian Terry was accordingly found not guilty on the grounds of diminished responsibility. But when he heard the verdict, he shouted, 'Oh but I am guilty! What have they brought me in not guilty for?'

James Sargisson and Joseph Myers 1864

The shambolic execution of James Sargisson and Joseph Myers was the only public execution to take place outside the jail at Armley. Myers was unusual in that he had tried to cheat death by cutting his throat while on death row; his life was saved by the surgeon. The *Leeds Mercury* claimed that 80,000 to 100,000 people had come to gawp and gloat at the execution that Saturday morning. At five to nine, the prison bell began to toll while the two men were being pinioned by York hangman Thomas Askern. The convicts continued to chat with each other as Askern pulled down the white caps over their faces: Sargisson's last words to Myers were 'Art thou happy lad?' to which Myers replied 'Indeed I am.' Askern then operated the drop: Myers seemed to die almost at once, but Sargisson struggled for some minutes: suffering excruciating pain in the extreme. To add to the spectacle, the wound in Myers' throat had reopened and there was blood visible all over his shirt. After hanging for the customary hour, they were taken down from the gallows and buried within the prison.

Eli Sykes 1865

Eli Sykes was buried next to Sargisson and Myers in Armley, but under very different circumstances. As a suicide, Sykes was buried at midnight with no religious ceremony – 'a shameful burial'. In early times suicide, or *felo de se*, was punishable by forfeiture of property to the monarch and a shameful burial – usually with a stake driven through the heart and at a crossroad, traditionally a satanic place, with no mourners or clergy present. Children or mentally compromised people, however, were not punished so severely post-mortem.

Nineteen year old Sykes qualified for the second category. He had murdered his girlfriend, Hannah Brook, eighteen, in Batley and, when he got to court, delivered a passionate, if somewhat prolix, address of supreme theatricality. To make matters worse, he had also stabbed Hannah's 60 year old mother to death and attempted to slash his own throat.

A defence of crime of passion was rejected by the jury and despite a desperate effort to avoid the noose by getting confirmed, Sykes was sentenced to hang in Armley Gaol. But it was not to be: he hurled himself the 30 feet down over the prison's second floor banister and landed on the stone floor – on his feet – surviving but shattering his left foot. Furious that his suicide attempt had failed he proceeded to bang his head repeatedly on the floor until restrained by four warders. Sykes was hallucinating at this point – haunted by visions of Hannah before him.

He was buried in the dead of night – a shameful burial for a shameful act.

Thomas Midgeley 1865

This became known as the Hanging Ditch murder. Sarah Dawson and the murderer's father discovered the body of Thomas Midgeley's wife who had sustained severe knife wounds and was virtually decapitated. Up until the dreadful event, the couple had enjoyed a model marriage, although Midgeley had been reported as acting rather oddly of late.

Midgeley was a mule piecer and overlooker at Fielden's Mill, Todmorden. On Christmas Day 1863, he married Mary Ann Kershaw at Heptonstall Church; she was a weaver at Fielden's Mill. On 27th January 1865, he murdered Mary Ann at Hanging Ditch, Todmorden. Around 11.00 am on that morning, scuffles and screams were heard coming from the Midgleys' house. Midgley was found holding up his bloody hands; he said 'I have done it. I have done it'. When he was arrested, he told the police that he meant to kill her the previous night with a razor, but an angel came and took it from him. He had written a rambling letter which read: 'Thomas Midgley and Mary Ann Kershaw, this is my last duty in this world, and before I leave it I warn the world of the folly of sin. The Almighty has laid his hand upon her and myself because of my sin and wickedness. He has been just and kind to me… Then my sins are more numerous than the hairs on my head and the consciousness of my own folly has made me crazy but thou hast been just and kind. But I have been a wicked sinner and there is nothing to look for in this world but misery and woe. The Almighty has laid a curse upon me and there is my hope either in this world or in the next but my wife has been an angel of light and I am to stand the hard wrath of god in the fire'.

The inquest at the Golden Lion in Todmorden returned a verdict of wilful murder; Midgley was tried at Leeds Assizes and acquitted on the grounds of insanity and ordered to be confined during Her Majesty's Pleasure.

Israel Blum 1866

When Bradford school teacher Israel Blum caught a train to Liverpool in 1866 it was generally agreed that he was acting very much out of character. His body was found in Wallasey; he had been murdered. Before leaving Bradford, Blum had bought a copy of Charles Dickens' *David Copperfield*. The book was found next to his body, the page referring to a 'northern murder' had been folded over.

The Murder of Lawrence Donaghey 1866

Drink-fuelled fights were not unusual in industrial Middlesbrough in the latter part of the 19th century. A policeman heard sounds of a disturbance and a woman's screams at 65 Stockton Street but took no action because this was not unusual in the locality. When he passed by again, the screams were still coming from the house: he entered to find Lawrence Donaghey lying bleeding and dead on the floor with two wounds to his head; his mother was screaming. The house was home to nine people – the Donagheys and two lodgers.

Lawrence had been let in by his mother: he was not injured at the time, possibly drunk; Mrs. Donaghey was sober. At 12.30 a.m. they were awakened by a noise and found Lawrence dead. One of the lodgers, Owen Collins, initially told police that there was no discord in the family but later, at the Middlesbrough Town Hall inquest, changed his story and said there were frequent rows – mainly about drink and money; Lawrence was the only breadwinner and he was accused of not handing enough money over for the housekeeping. Samuel Crowther, a neighbour at No. 69, heard rowing and two women pleading 'don't murder poor Larry, it will be a bad job'. The women were Lawrence's mother and an older sister. The domestic rows were confirmed by Crowther and another neighbour, Susan Bartley.

That fateful night Lawrence had first gone to the George and Dragon and then the Liberal Beerhouse in Stockton Street; he left both increasingly drunk but the landlord of the beerhouse had his nephew, James Miller, take Lawrence home. Miller passed him over to Lawrence's mother who took him inside. Later investigations revealed no blood on Lawrence's hat, or on any of the furniture in the house which Lawrence may have fallen against. The examiners concluded that Lawrence died from a fractured skull caused by something heavy, like a poker, or by a kick from a boot. Due to the conflicting and inconclusive evidence, a verdict of 'murder by some person or persons unknown' was returned.

Ann Hinchcliffe 1867

There are many repellent and disturbing cases of murder in this book, but this one involving Ann Hinchcliffe's murder of her grandchild must rank as one of the most atrocious. Hinchcliffe, from Knottingley, used a vegetable poison resembling creosote to end the child's life. She was acquitted: an astonishing verdict when it was known by the jury that she had sent her grandson to purchase the 'creosote' used over a number of visits to the shop, that she had described the child as 'an encumbrance' and that Hinchcliffe herself, being the grandmother, could never plead mitigation through the effects of puerperal depression.

The grandchild was the illegitimate son of Christiana Speed. When the baby died it was nailed up in a nailbox – Christiana traded in nails – and delivered to Knottingley Cemetery by John Barber, a clog maker lodger at the house and Christiana's brother-in-law. The baby was handed over as a stillbirth boy with the name William Roberts, the same name as the putative father of the baby. The baby was buried by Jane Sawyer, the sexton's niece; her uncle was out of town and Sawyer believed she was burying a stillborn baby boy. Suspicions were raised, however, about what was in effect an unregistered birth and an unregistered death for which no doctor had been called: the infant was exhumed.

The subsequent postmortem revealed hydrogen chloride in the child's stomach – in use today as a drain cleaner and industrial paint remover. The gastrointestinal tract was severely burned. Hydrogen chloride forms corrosive hydrochloric acid on contact with water found in body tissue. Hinchcliffe's poison resembled creosote. Hinchcliffe claimed that Christiana, her daughter, not her, had administered the poison by mistake, confusing it with spirit of salt.

Both Ann and Christiana were charged with murder at Leeds Assizes. Christiana confessed that her mother had said they had better smother the child as they could not find the father. Charges against Christiana were dropped and Anna walked free after a unanimous 'not guilty' verdict. The vendors of the creosote were never called and the jury believed that the poisoning was accidental because salt was genuinely, it seems, confused with creosote.

Catherine O'Brien 1867

Catherine O'Brien had two children, Mary Ann who was thirteen, and Michael who was one month old. Her husband had recently deserted them for a life in the United States, taking with him all the family's money. It was a full house in Cannon Street, Middlesbrough: apart from the three O'Briens, two cousins Thomas and Ellen Conaugh and an aunt also lived there. Early one Sunday morning Mary Ann was holding the baby and, oddly, told Thomas the baby was going to die. Catherine took the baby into her bed, where, sure enough, it died. No surgeon was called until the Sunday afternoon. An inquest was held at the Volunteer Hotel in Cannonfield, Middlesbrough where it was established that baby Michael had died from suffocation. It also emerged that Catherine was unable to breastfeed Michael and that Mary Ann had kissed the baby on the mouth for which she was chastised and slapped by her mother. Attempts to revive the child were unsuccessful. The coroner suspected that suffocation was caused by the mother 'overlaying' the baby, and not by any kissing; but there was no real evidence to establish a definitive cause of death. Catherine and Mary Ann got off with warnings.

Miles Weatherill 1868

Sixteen year old Sarah Bell went to Todmorden from her home in York to work as a cook for the Reverend Anthony Plow. She attracted the attention of weaver Miles Weatherill who lived in Back Brook Street; Reverend Plow was displeased by the relationship his young cook was having and fired her, sending her back to York. Weatherill was furious, visited her at her mother's home at Newby Whiske, near Thirsk and returned on March 2nd to murder Plow, after fortifying himself in the Black Swan. He was armed with four pistols and an axe.

The carnage started with an attack on the Reverend Plow who managed to escape with a deep gash in his skull delivered by the axe when one of the pistols failed to fire. Three women servants – Elizabeth Spink, Mary Hodgson, and Jane Smith came to Plow's aid. Weatherill struck Jane Smith with the axe, almost severing her hand, then shot her dead. He then dashed upstairs where he shot Mrs. Harriet Plow, the vicar's wife who was in bed with her baby. He shot at her beneath the sheets at which she leapt out of bed but Weatherill battered her with a poker and left her for dead.

Reverend Plow died on 12th March 1868, and his five-week-old daughter, Hilda Katherine, died that the same day. The press put it about that she died from the 'unavoidable removal from its mother at the time of the attack on her'. Mrs. Plow died a year later. Weatherill was convicted of the wilful murder of Jane Smith at Manchester Assizes; he was hanged outside the New Bailey Prison, Manchester.

Frederick Parker 1868

The first thing you did when released from Beverley jail was to go into the Red Lion for a pint, or two. That is what Frederick Parker, a bricklayer all the way from Tottenham, did; Daniel Driscoll, from near Selby, did the same and the two ex-convicts got drunk together on a pub crawl that ended in Bubwith, eighteen miles from Beverley. Tactlessly, Driscoll disclosed that he was carrying over £4 on him. Parker acted on this information by beating Driscoll on the head with a hedgestake and relieved him of the £4 and his watch. Parker was the last man to hang in public at York.

Charlotte Barton 1870

Charlotte Barton was an unusual murderess in that she used a blunt instrument rather than the usual woman's weapon of choice: poison. We learn of her motive in a statement she gave while languishing in Broadmoor and attempting to secure her release: '[She] says the man whom she killed…was a "regular old rogue" that he took four pounds which she had laid by, and that she accused him of taking the money and … he struck her, and then she struck him in return with a hammer and knocked him down the … steps. She says that she had lived with him thirteen years – that she first went to do his washing and then he asked her to get married to him and keep his house. It is stated also that he wished her to lead an immoral life. She says she had been so low spirited for a long time that she did not know what to do'.

The man she killed was 57 year old Thomas Pagdin whom she murdered with a hammer and then pushed him down the cellar steps of their home in Sheffield. Pagdin had suffered seven major injuries: the *Illustrated Police News* reported that 'one eye was upturned, the other closed up…the face on both sides was pounded into a mass of pulp and the head was dreadfully mangled'.

Barton was eventually released into the care of her sister in 1886 aged sixty-two.

Matthew Cook 1871

Matthew Cook was a York watchmaker who had a mental breakdown one day when he was forty-five. He took his wife Sally and their young child out into countryside along Haxby Road where he literally went mad. He stabbed Sally more than 50 times and unsuccessfully tried to cut his own throat; all the while his child looked on in what must have been abject horror. Before he collapsed, bleeding profusely, on his wife's body, he was reported as jumping up and down singing 'Sally's the girl for me'. He tried to cover her body with soil. He later stated that he thought his wife had been unfaithful. On the way to Heworth he boasted that 'I have killed one of the best women in England. She took a hell of a lot of killing. She was fresh from the country'.

The press reported that 'a fiendish passion' had seized Matthew Cook before he murdered his wife and he was described as an obsessive husband prone to acts of jealous voyeurism. At Cook's trial, during which the defendant calmly pinched snuff throughout, the defence used *delirium tremens* (DT) and the alcoholism associated with it, and evidence of hereditary psychiatric problems to convince the jury he was insane.

Richard Gray 1871

The hazards of working as a prostitute are many, as are the records of women who fell victim to these hazards. The murder of Liz Shepherd in Bradford is a case in point. She was hurled from a window in a building at the junction of Manchester Road and Little Horton Road and died instantaneously. Liz had gone up to a workshop in the building which was owned by one of the three men who were with her, Barraclough, Gray and Harte. A known prostitute, she had met them in the nearby Queen's Hotel. The plan was clearly to drink beer and whisky and have group sex; they took with them a gallon of beer and whisky. The festivities could be heard on the street below; indeed a Constable Bower heard a man say 'Make less noise or I'll fettle your canister for you', followed by a woman's scream. He then witnessed a woman scrabbling about on the window sill then falling to her death. Forensics showed that Liz had been punched, that there had been a struggle and then she was forced out of the window. There was blood on the walls and stairs. Gray was convicted of wilful murder.

Death on the Haxby Road, York. *Illustrated Police News.*

Elizabeth Shepherd falls to her death when a sex party goes badly wrong. *Illustrated Police News*.

The Leven Carr Poisoning 1871

Assumption of guilt based on little or no real evidence must have been the death of many an innocent suspect. The case of 19 year old Hannah Bromby and her brush with the gallows illustrates this well in Leven Carr near Beverley. On May 19th 1871, the bodies of Matilda Harper, aged 50, and her four year old granddaughter, Lilly Taylor, were removed from Harper's farm – both had been poisoned. Servant girl Bromby was the chief suspect; she was accused of pouring red lead into the stream, a kettle was seen to froth and Matilda Harper complained of feeling sick after drinking water from the pump. When his wife and granddaughter died, Mr. Harper concluded that Bromby was the killer and accused her of poisoning them with arsenic.

The problem for Bromby was that Harper wielded power and influence locally; Bromby had neither. The common factor in the deaths was tea which was drunk by the two deceased and a farm labourer, Henry Dunn, who also exhibited symptoms of arsenic poisoning. Bromby had made the tea so she was arrested on a charge of murder. The victims' organs revealed the presence of arsenic as did water from the kettle used to brew the tea. The pump water was clear but vomit found outside from Mrs. Harper contained arsenic. A complicating factor, though, for the prosecution was that Bromby had been told to fill the kettle from the stream rather than the pump because of the froth coming from the kettle. There was no real evidence to convict Bromby, just assumptions. The case was dropped until such time as new evidence might emerge.

George Henry Bishop 1871

When George Bishop, his father Joseph, his brother and a worker called Jonathan Mitchell, were bringing in the harvest one day in 1871 at Dore near Sheffield they could have had no idea that a grim reaper was to make an appearance. George's father began to criticise his scything skills and then started kicking and punching him. George retaliated with his scythe and struck his father with it. The blade entered his father's back just blow the left shoulder blade and exited through his chest, killing him. George handed himself in, stating that he was provoked and 'let my scythe slip through my hands'. The jury at the trial responded by not letting Bishop slip and returned a verdict of manslaughter.

Charles Sleight 1871

All murders are cruel, but this one plumbed new depths of depravity. Charles Sleight, 30 years old and a respected teacher at the East Riding and Lincolnshire Deaf and Dumb Institution at 10 Dock Street in Hull, found himself in a cell at Hull Prison accused of murdering Maria Hailstone, a deaf and dumb woman aged 24. John Hailstone, Maria's husband, a house painter by trade, also deaf and dumb, went to stay with his in-laws, unable to bear being at his flat at the Institution where his wife had had her throat cut with an open razor found at the scene. Maria Hailstone had been almost decapitated.

The morning of the atrocity, John had left for work in Hessle. Charles Sleight lodged with them and was still in his bedroom on the floor below the couple's bedroom when John left. Charles had been complaining of headaches, although he managed the night before to give a talk to a meeting at the Institution. Later that morning Charles went to the local police station in Parliament Street where he exhibited signs of anxiety, ripping up some papers on the desk and throwing them about before telling the police go to the Institution where they would find Maria's body. Sleight confessed that he was the murderer but not before he had threatened a policeman with a poker and was locked up 'for being in an insane state at the police station'.

A police search uncovered a blood-soaked nightshirt under a rug on the bed; a number of razors (John Hailstone did not use razors) and a recently oiled sharpening stone. Sleight was charged with murder and committed to York Assizes. It was later revealed that Sleight was attracted to Maria, had tried to kiss her and sat her on his knee. Maria had complained to her husband John about this, but John did nothing. Sleight divulged his feelings to a friend and the manager of the Institution, Thomas Haller, who told him to resolve the matter by marrying his girlfriend, a Miss Jacques from Brough, as soon as possible. The police surgeon who examined Maria's body found no evidence of Maria being raped. Pupils at the institute had noticed a change in Sleight's behaviour; he complained to his sister Jane who lived in Harrogate that he was homesick and lonely and that he was going out of his mind. Charles had consulted a doctor about persistent headaches who referred him onto another doctor for a second opinion. Unfortunately, Sleight murdered Maria before this second opinion could be given. There was a long and voluminous history of severe mental illness in the family.

At the trial the foreman of the jury stood up and told the judge that the jury did not need to hear any more evidence because their decision was clear: to acquit Sleight on the grounds of insanity. The judge agreed and ordered Sleight to be detained at Her Majesty's Pleasure. He was committed to Broadmoor Criminal Lunatic Asylum to join 628 other inmates described on the census return as 'criminal lunatics'.

Jane Crompton 1873

Soon after the birth of baby Sarah Alice, Jane Crompton told neighbours in Hull's Osborne Street that she was no good for her baby and that she was having difficulty breastfeeding, so resorted to a bottle. She often asked Alice Fox to wash and dress the baby for her, asserting that she did not like the child; how she couldn't touch it; how she would never bring it up; and how good it would be if she were in heaven. Later she confided to Alice Fox that she was going to do something to the baby, to which the neighbour replied that 'they will tickle you up for it'. Alice became increasingly concerned and frequently called in to check on both mother and baby, taking reassurance that her husband was a good husband and that all would turn out well.

Tragically, when her husband John had left for work on May 15th 1873 she went next door to Alice Fox to tell her that 'I have done something to baby'. Her other daughter, Bertha, was with her and chimed in with utterly disarming candour: 'I watched mother take a key out of her pocket and unlock dada's box. She took dada's knife out and cut Alice's head off and laid it on the kilt [quilt]'. Alice Fox went back to the Crompton's house and witnessed a scene of unspeakable carnage. Naturally, she became hysterical and terrified for the safety of her own four children.

PC Dixey attended the scene; Crompton was arrested but not before an angry mob had gathered, one of which tried to stab Crompton with a knife. Jane Crompton admitted the crime. The sickening rumour mill lurched into action with stories that Jane combed the decapitated head, dressed the torso and invited neighbours in to see how pretty Sarah Alice looked. Bertha was reputedly the child of a former lover, hence her affection for Bertha.

Whatever, Jane Crompton blamed her actions on the treatment meted out to her by neighbours Alice Fox and Mrs. Wood, and on her depressive state. The inquest was held in the Tynemouth Castle public house. Jane's sanity was never questioned and she was convicted of wilful murder to which she pleading guilty; but the prosecution conceded that she was in a depressed state of mind when she committed the act and the judge urged the defence to persuade her to change her plea to not guilty on the grounds that she was suffering from melancholia. She was found not guilty of murder on the grounds of insanity and detained at Her Majesty's Pleasure.

Annie Costello 1873

Annie Costello, a factory girl from Halifax, can only be described as bordering on the feral. She spent all of her wages on alcohol which usually precipitated arguments and violence. One evening in 1873 she staggered home to her boarding house and proceeded to argue with two lodgers. Her father was appalled and intervened, twisting Annie's hair and slapping her face. Annie grabbed a pitcher and a rolling pin; her father wrested the pitcher from her but was unable to stop her beating him about the head with the rolling pin. He collapsed under the table but she first sank her nails into his tongue and then wrenched it hard. Mr. Costello was in considerable agony and died next day in the workhouse hospital asphyxiated by his swelling tongue. Annie was convicted of manslaughter and sentenced to ten years imprisonment.

Henry Shaw 1873

Mary Ward was a 40 year old transient – slightly unusual because most transient people were men. She was married but separated. On Christmas Eve 1873 she arrived in Carlin How, a village in between Loftus and Skinningrove near Redcar. She called in at the pub there, got drunk and left. Unfortunately for Mary, 19 year old Henry Shaw, Joseph Carter and James Fleming were lying in wait for her. They knocked her about, Carter threw a pale of water over her, and they took her into a field where she was raped. Her screams for help went ignored. Next morning her body was found at the bottom of the Lofthouse Iron Company mine shaft. A hairpin, bonnet and other of her items were found in the field. A medical examination showed one arm, spine and both legs were fractured while her right elbow was dislocated; these would have been sustained in the fall down the shaft. In addition there was severe bruising on the face and body which occurred before the fall. Shaw, Carter and Fleming were soon apprehended but the latter two were found not guilty of all charges. Shaw was sentenced to ten years' penal servitude.

William Jackson 1874

Jackson, from Carthorpe near Bedale, killed his sister. He was ex-army, having served in India, and now lived at home. After a row he was thrown out; his doting sixteen year old sister, Elizabeth, insisted on going with him; in a fit of madness on the road to Ripon he cut her throat, nearly decapitating her. Jackson's lawyers lodged a plea of temporary insanity caused by the effect of the sun while he was in India, but this failed and he was hanged at York – the first private hanging there. On that fateful day, the Jacksons lost the second of their two children within a few weeks of each other.

William Smedley 1875

The first private execution at Armley Gaol was that of 54 year old William Smedley from Sheffield. Something a girlfriend of his, Elizabeth Firth, had said made the drunken Smedley snap and cut her throat with a razor. He fled the scene but soon gave himself up.

The General Tarleton Murder 1876

In 1876 The General Tarleton pub was the scene of an alcohol fuelled disturbance which was to have fatal consequences for the landlord, Robert Gibson. On the morning of May 22nd four thirsty militiamen from the 5th Yorkshire Militia turned up and ordered a quart of beer. When it came to pay they were reluctant to stand the 6d charged and said they would only pay 4d. Gibson protested and refused to serve them any more beer. The militiamen became rowdy and started singing and dancing but eventually left without further trouble. However, they came back, a fight later ensued and Gibson was hit by one of the soldiers, Bartley, striking his head on the ground – a trauma which obviously incapacitated him. He was carried back into the General Tarleton and lapsed into a coma; he died the following morning. An inquest at the Blue Bell Inn in Arkendale found Bartley guilty of manslaughter; he was sentenced at Leeds to seven years penal servitude.

The General Tarleton was the scene of an inquest in March 1881 when the body of a baby was found in the icy village pond. It was discovered by Arthur Wade, the 14 year old son of the innkeeper Robert Wade, while he was out breaking the ice. The baby girl was face-down, muddied, naked and was in eight inches of water; she had been there for some days. The coroner, William Renton, could find no obvious signs of violence; the post mortem confirmed that the child was dead before she entered the water; the mystery surrounding her fate remains to this day.

John Henry Johnson 1877

John Henry Johnson, 37, was unfortunate to be the victim of another botched execution as reported by the *Yorkshire Post* on Wednesday the 3rd April 1877. Johnson had been convicted of the murder of Amos Waite who had been showing an over-enthusiastic interest in Johnson's wife, Amelia, on Boxing Day 1876. There was a drink-fuelled quarrel in the pub; Johnson went home, and then came back armed with a gun: he shot Waite in the chest. Thomas Askern was brought from York to Leeds to execute Johnson but when he pulled the lever the rope snapped and Johnson hurtled down through the trap. He was quickly rescued by the warders who removed his straps and hood and sat him down on a chair. Askern took ten agonising minutes to rig up a new rope and reset the trap before Johnson could be led up onto it again. This time the rope held but Johnson reportedly 'died hard', struggling for four minutes on the rope. His death was formally recorded as being from asphyxia; no mention was made of the botched first attempt. This was Askern's last execution at Armley.

Anthony Owston 1878

'I will cut thy throat an' all and then my own!' These were the frightening words which greeted grocer John Smith when Owston dashed into his Bradford shop wielding a blade, slashing at the air and Smith's arms. Smith was saved by his assistant who formed a human shield between the two men. When he said 'an' all' Owston was making it clear that he had already cut the throat of another victim; that victim was his wife, Jane, who had a drink problem and was accused by her insanely jealous husband for spending too much time with Smith as a frequent customer for the alcohol he sold.

This is what happened that evening of 28th September 1878: Owston was at home in Bradford with Jane, their children, and Jane's mother. Jane went upstairs, and a 'distressed' Owston said to his mother-in-law 'I cannot live without Jane. I loved her as a boy and I love her as a man.' He then got up, and followed Jane upstairs. Jane came down to the kitchen bleeding profusely from the neck where she collapsed and died. Owston then made his way to John Smith's shop next door; he had heard Jane scream, locked his doors and hid under the counter, but Owston 'bounded through a small window' into the shop and attacked him.

Thwarted in his attempt to slay Smith, Owston did indeed cut his own throat; he then staggered home only to find policemen there investigating his wife's death. He was arrested and confessed, explaining his actions with a note which read: 'I loved her dearly … She said she would leave me … I've been jealous some time … I have been certain they intended to run away. I am guilty, and I hope she is dead … She has been determined to leave me. Let me die. I've begged of her to live with me, as I could not give her up'.

The press reported how Owston was taken to Bradford Infirmary where his mental condition became so much worse – he being subject to fits of despondency – that it was deemed prudent in the interests of the other patients in the Infirmary, who were terrified by his strange conduct, to remove him to the lunatic wards at the Bradford Workhouse.

Owston was found not guilty on grounds of insanity and sent to Broadmoor Criminal Lunatic Asylum. Here a repentant Owston did his best to work hard in one of the workshops, as described in this letter he wrote to Superintendent William Orange: 'my only desire has been to give satisfaction in my work and also to earn as much money as I possibly could on account of the unfortunate position of my children. I assure you I have denied myself almost of everything in the shape of luxuries or anything else purposely to send all I earned home to enable my sisters to keep the home together, as it appears since my fathers death over two years ago they have had much to do to tide over their difficulties in providing for 4 children … you will see my only object now is to do what I can to assist my family and not consider myself'. But Owston's mental health continued to deteriorate: in the mid 1890s he 'was found in [day]room on window ledge trying to break the window. He had evedently [sic] fallen off as he has several bruises on his back, he had also scratched his throat, either with his nails or also a tin button. His scrotum was also bleeding and was scratched, he said God almighty had told him to destroy himself. At 1.15 he became very maniacal forced himself into the gallery and threw himself against the opposite window slightly cutting corner under left eye'. He lapsed into a coma but, against all expectations, recovered. His physical health improved, but his mental health just got worse: 'A. Owston troubled with religious mania. Says he asked God on chapel yesterday morning if he should sing, says after he could scarcely open his mouth, so that he could not sing. Says he had vision from God in the night that Mr. Gladstone and 10 others were killed in a railway accident, says whatever God tells him to do he shall do. Says if God was to tell [him] to cut his throat he must do it, says he hopes he will not tell him to do that for he wishes to live, as he is a changed man and feels younger and stronger than ever he did'.

By 1904 he was suffering 'chronic delusional insanity', and at the end of 1905 the asylum authorities informed his family that he was seriously ill. His son – resolutely supportive and one never to give up hope – replied: 'we sincerely trust he will yet take a turn for the better. It is unfortunate his … trouble has reappeared but we feel content to know that my father is in good hands and your good self and staff will do your best for him'. But, soon after, Owston died; cause of death: 'exhaustion following mania'. For many years after Owston's death, his children sent a wreath to Broadmoor at Christmas, Easter, and on the anniversary of his death to be placed upon his grave.

Vincent Walker 1878

When Vincent Walker crashed drunk into a butcher's shop in Hull's Nile Street with an axe under his arm, he was disarmed. When he walked into a Hull pub wielding a home-made sword, he was again disarmed. When he battered on the door of a Mrs. White carrying a knife, there was to be no disarming. He had gone there to give his estranged wife some cockles; Mrs. White had taken Mrs. Walker in; unfortunately, she let slip that Vincent Walker's wife was upstairs with another man. Walker battered Mrs. White to death, stabbed her and threatened any interfering neighbours with the same treatment. When arrested and brought back to the crime scene he managed to kick Mrs. White's corpse, pronouncing that if his wife had been there she would have got 'the same dose'. William Marwood did the honours at York – the second private hanging. Unfortunately, it was another botch with the victim writhing for five minutes after the bolt was released.

Charles Peace 1879

Charlie Peace was a career criminal with a series of burglaries and two murders to his inglorious name by the time he was hanged in Armley Gaol in 1879. He had been permanently crippled in an accident at a steel-rolling mill and had already spent a number of stretches in jail before the murders. In 1875, Peace moved into the Sheffield suburb of Darnall where he met Mr. and Mrs. Dyson and allegedly began an affair with Mrs. Dyson. They certainly went out together to music halls and pubs but she rebuffed his sexual advances which displeased Peace who threatened to 'blow out the brains' of Mr. and Mrs. Dyson. Dyson, a civil engineer, promptly took out an injunction against Peace who moved to Hull and opened a café. The Dysons, meanwhile, later moved to the leafy suburb of Bannercross.

While living in Hull Peace went to Manchester, armed as usual with his revolver and was spotted by two policemen loitering near a house at Whalley Range, around midnight on the 1st of August 1876. Constable Nicholas Cock tried to arrest him but Peace produced the revolver and told Cock to back off, firing a warning shot at the officer. Cock drew his truncheon and advanced towards Peace, who fired again, killing him. Peace escaped back to Hull; two local villains, brothers John and William Habron, were arrested for the crime. John was acquitted through lack of evidence; William Habron was convicted and sentenced to death but, fortunately as it happened, this was commuted to penal servitude and life imprisonment. Peace enjoyed the trial from the public gallery.

Peace was still intent on Mrs. Dyson and to that end he continued to stalk her; he went to the Dysons' new home at Bannercross where Mrs. Dyson was accosted by Peace, who said "You see, I am here to annoy you, and I'll annoy you wherever you go." That evening he returned saying to Mrs. Dyson as she made her way to an outhouse, "Speak or I'll fire." Mr. Dyson came out; Peace shot Mr. Dyson through the head, killing him instantly, after which he escaped back to Hull by train. Mrs. Dyson, however, identified him as her husband's killer. A £100 reward was offered and Peace was now the nation's most wanted man moving from one place to another, evading capture for over two years. The police issued a description that was so inaccurate it had to be altered, but Peace was forever changing his appearance, even concealing his missing finger with a prosthetic arm. Peace set up as a music dealer in London as a front for his night job – house burglary – and sometimes carried his tools in a violin case. He was now living comfortably in Peckham with a Susan Thompson, real name Susan Bailey, the woman who finally betrayed him, and his son, Willie. He masqueraded as an inventor, even patenting a device for raising sunken vessels for which he was interviewed at the House of Commons.

Peace was finally apprehended by three policeman in Blackheath in the throes of robbing a house: he fired several shots wounding PC Robinson in the arm before he was overpowered. When questioned he gave his name as John Ward. Susan Thompson was also arrested for attempting to sell stolen property and identified Ward as Peace. Peace stood trial at the Old Bailey in November 1878 on the charges of burglary and attempted murder of the three policemen and was sentenced to life in prison.

That still left the murder of Mr. Dyson; Peace was taken twice by train to Sheffield to be charged with the murder of Arthur Dyson. En route the second time he tried to escape by throwing himself out of a train window but was quickly recaptured, lying unconscious by the side of the track. At his trial at Leeds Assizes, ballistic forensic evidence proved that the bullet which killed Mr. Dyson was fired from the revolver recovered from Peace when he was arrested in London. The jury retired and took a mere ten minutes to convict him. While awaiting execution, he confessed to the murder of PC Cock: William Habron was pardoned and awarded £800 compensation. Peace claimed again that Mrs. Dyson had been his mistress – a claim which she refuted calling him a devil, "beyond the power of even a Shakespeare to paint". Peace's final words were "My last thoughts are for children and their mother, a wonderful woman, they mustn't worry about me I know where I am going. I am going to Heaven." A tableau of Peace and Marwood, the hangman, soon starred in Madame Tussaud's depicting the execution scene. Mrs. Dyson emigrated to Cleveland, Ohio at the end of the trial.

Richard Gaukroger 1880

Richard Gaukroger, 31, lived with his wife, Harriet, on the York Road in east Leeds. Richard spent much of his time in the pub, a pursuit for which he was constantly harangued by Harriet. In time he grew tired of this and decided he wanted to spend the rest of his life with another woman called Poll. He raised this with Harriet who responded by raising the poker to him and threatening him with it. Richard was smoking a pipe at the time and snapped, dashing across the room and ramming the pipe stem up into her nose. Harriet gingerly withdrew the pipe which resulted in extreme pain and profuse bleeding. For his part, Richard reclaimed the pipe and resumed smoking it. Unfortunately, over the next few days, Harriet deteriorated and then died. The post mortem showed a fragment of the pipe lodged in her skull; cause of death was inflammation of the brain. Richard Gawkroger was convicted of manslaughter and 21 months in jail.

Kate Dover 1880

Twenty-seven year old Felicia Dorothea Kate Dover ran a sweet shop in Sheffield's London Road; she lived with her parents in Thirlwell Terrace, Heeley. Her father was a wood carver. Kate was a free spirit, an unusually independent woman, notable for her fashionable clothes and a liking for the finer things in life. Kate Dover was 'the Queen of Heeley'.

Kate became attracted to a local man living at 24 Glover Street – Thomas Skinner, an artist and etcher and something of a bohemian. He had invented a new method of etching designs onto steel and bone which enabled the mass production of designs on cutlery and razors, a very useful skill in a place like Sheffield. At 61 years of age he was more than 30 years older than Kate. Her parents had misgivings but the two became an item and then got engaged. Kate gave up her shop and became his housekeeper, displacing the previous housekeeper, Mrs. Jones.

On the 5th of December 1881 Kate bought an ounce of arsenic to colour some artificial flowers from a chemist in Abbeydale Road, and then met Thomas Skinner in The Big Tree at Woodseats. There was talk of buying Kate a pony with the couple looking forward to their wedding the following March. At the chemist, Kate had complied with the procedure whereby a witness was required to sign and witness the purchase; this though was after Kate had already sent a girl out to buy some laudanum and chloroform and came back empty handed because the chemists, Learoyd's, required some guarantees of user and use.

Back at the house, dinner was roast chicken and stuffing. On the following afternoon, Dr. Harrison was called from his London Road surgery to Glover Street to find the couple experiencing burning in their mouths and a bloating in the stomach. Thomas was rather more serious than Kate, and said "She has done for us both this time" suggesting that the vegetables sent by his former housekeeper, Mrs. Jones, and used by Kate to make the stuffing had somehow been adulterated. The doctor was sure this was a case of arsenic poisoning and took away samples of the meal to be analysed. Tests later showed that the chicken was contaminated with arsenic but the stuffing was clear. Kate had only eaten the stuffing but had vomited all the same. Thomas died.

There were, inevitably, rumours about the stormy relationship the couple had, with arguments over the lack of money, accusations that Kate had pawned some of Thomas's clothes to feed her shopping habit, and of assaults by Thomas on Kate, and of love letters written by Kate to another man. Kate was arrested on suspicion of murder and appeared at Leeds Assizes.

There Kate Dover was found guilty of manslaughter because the jury was reluctant to sentence a woman to hang, and there was no apparent motive. Moreover, she had everything to gain by prolonging the relationship with Thomas. The judge, who was looking for a murder verdict, sentenced her to life: the first woman to be sentenced to penal servitude for life. By 1901 she was out, living with her sister in Rotherham.

Thomas Beckett 1880

When Mrs. Beckett left Thomas Beckett, a labourer at Hemsworth Colliery near their home in Walton, close to Wakefield, things were unbearable enough. But when he saw her with Harry Ogden, that was just too much. Ill advisedly, after the sighting she was persuaded by Beckett to go back to the cottage, where, apparently, she agreed a suicide pact with her estranged husband 'to do each other'. And that is what, according to Thomas Beckett, they did. Mrs. Beckett assaulted her husband with a blunt kitchen knife while Mr. Beckett returned the favour with something much sharper – a razor. She was dead but he was forced to try and finish himself off with said razor. He failed.

The committal judge directed the jury to find Beckett guilty of murder which they did; at the assizes the jury found him guilty of the lesser charge of manslaughter due to the extreme provocation he had endured. He was sentenced to four days imprisonment.

Bridget O'Rourke 1880

A long marriage is no guarantee of marital harmony, as Thomas O'Rourke was to discover at his house in No. 3, Court 2 Home Tippet Lane in Sheffield. Thomas was counting his money one Saturday night when Bridget, his wife, suggested strongly that he was hiding some from her. He denied this, adding that it was all for her anyway. She then picked up a paraffin lamp and hurled it at Thomas: it exploded in his face, burning his face and chest and his hands when he struggled to loosen a burning scarf that was tightly tied around his neck. Bridget's efforts to douse the flames were in vain. Thomas died of his wounds, but not before he had made a generous statement on his deathbed defending Bridget and the 40 years of strife free marriage they had enjoyed. She was convicted of manslaughter.

Osmond Otto Brand 1881

This shocking case involves some of the most repellent systematic brutality and sadism ever recorded in a British court of law. Twenty-seven year old Brand, skipper of a fishing smack, was convicted of the murder of William Papper, a fisher boy, aged fifteen years, while in the North Sea, and was sentenced to death at the Yorkshire Assize at Leeds. It seems to have all started when *The Rising Sun* left Hull: as Papper boarded the vessel on the 16th December, Brand was saying farewell to Hannah his wife.

Papper, innocuously said to Brand, "Skipper, my sister says she knows you", which suggested there had been a relationship, but a remark all the same which seemed to have infuriated Brand who later threatened, "As soon as I got you out I'll kill you."

Ninety miles off Spurn Point the shocking litany of torture began. Brand first sent Papper below for some spurious reason, followed him and beat him with a length of rope about the head, face and body for ten minutes or so, causing his nose to bleed and his face to swell painfully. This was resumed that evening and continued until 23rd December, when the boy was ordered to stand on the stem of the vessel in a rolling sea and extreme winter weather; Papper was made to stand there for two hours all the while pelted with stones and mud dredged from the sea bed. Whilst the boy was lying on the deck, Brand threw buckets of cold water on him then he beat him with a stick, leaving him moaning and unable to move or speak.

On Christmas Eve the brutality continued when Brand also tied a rope round his neck threatening to hang him. He fastened the boy to the halyard, attached that to the winch, and ordered Blackburn, one of the other boys, to haul him up. Blackburn protested, but Brand threatened to shoot him. When Blackburn turned the winch, Brand grabbed Papper by the legs, and pulled until the crosstrees to which the halyard was attached broke, and the boy fell violently and senseless to the deck. Brand then beat him on the back of the neck and jumped on his chest.

On Christmas Day the crew enjoyed duck and plum pudding but Papper, who had been denied food for a number of days, was initially given nothing. When his dinner was finally taken up to him, Brand gave it to the dog, and handed Papper a solitary currant on a fork. When the dog had eaten the meat, Brand threw the bones to the boy.

The barbarity continued apace for three more days; Papper was forced to stand at the stern in a biting frost while Brand threw buckets of water over him. On the Thursday morning, Papper went down into the hold: Brand again threw a bucketful of water over him, and then dragged him up by a rope. Brand punched him between the eyes while Rycroft, the third mate, stuffed filthy sludge from the bilge into his mouth. He was then lashed to a railing while yet more water was thrown over him. Later, Brand lowered him into the dill, a filthy place full of bilge water. There Rycroft tied a rope under Papper's arms while Brand got on the boy shoulders, making him sink under the fetid water. He was hauled up and again dropped into the water. When Papper was back on deck, Brand beat him with a heavy stick, jumped on him, and again ordered water to be thrown over him. Brand then ordered Papper to be stitched into a piece of canvas with only his head protruding; he was lowered into the freezing sea and hauled back on deck when Brand said, "He's done – haul him out." A few minutes later Papper died. Brand hid the body in a bunk, and later threw the body into the sea, pretending that the boy had been knocked overboard by the foresail sheet.

Brand's story held good for two months until the other members of the crew, Dench, Blackburn and Yates, reported what really had happened to the Hull police. Brand, who was in Hull at the time, was arrested, and Rycroft, who was then at sea, was taken into custody on returning to shore. Brand was charged with the wilful murder of Papper on the high seas and was hanged at Armley Gaol. Rycroft pleaded guilty to common assault, and was sentenced to three months' hard labour.

John Critchley 1881

One morning in 1881 two miners, Peter Kelley and his son, were on their way to work in Batley as usual when they saw a sack on the doorstep of a butcher's shop in the High Street. Inside was the bloated body of John Critchley; his feet were tied and he was half naked. A Mary Wigglesworth lived at the shop, Critchley's girlfriend; a photo of her was found on his body along with some pawn tickets. Critchley had been a successful card maker but had fallen from grace and became a victim, presumably of his new-found low life associates.

Joseph Laycock 1884

When Joseph Laycock, a hawker, married Maria Green in 1875 the marriage, and Maria, were doomed from the start. Laycock was an intemperate man with a history of drink-related violence, exhibited especially towards Maria; Maria took to drink to soften the blows and to help raise the four children they had by 1884 at their home in White Croft, Sheffield. But the drink just made her violent too. In 1879 Laycock was arrested on suspicion of stabbing a man; he also had a reputation as a prize fighter. Joseph had actually tried to kill Maria twice. In June 1884 he was sentenced to 21 days in prison for assaulting and beating Maria but this changed nothing because the violence continued.

The following is paraphrased from *The Times* report of the trial, August 6th 1884: When Laycock was brought up he cried bitterly, but as the trial went on he gradually became calmer, but throughout the proceedings he kept his head buried in his hands. The details of the case were terrible. The prisoner lived with his wife Maria Laycock in Sheffield. They had four children – Sarah Ann aged 8 years; Francis George aged six years; Mary Ann aged four years and Joseph aged two years.

The proceedings on the day of the murder went something like this: Maria spent the morning collecting empty medicine bottles to earn some cash but she started drinking after midday. Late that afternoon she was confronted by her mother at The Warm Hearthstone Inn in Townhead Street who accused her of wasting money on drink while neglecting her hungry children. On hearing this the landlord refused to serve her and evicted her. She was next seen fighting with a woman in Hawley Croft and at 6 o'clock a witness saw Joseph collecting Maria from another pub which culminated in a street fight between the couple. The prisoner saw a police constable and Laycock shouted "She's been drinking with another man. Take her in and me an' all" The policeman told them to go home at which point Joseph went home to feed the children. Maria went to her mother's and with her brother Christopher went to Glossop Road to sell the medicine bottles they had collected. On the way home it rained heavily so Maria and Christopher called in at the Bearder's pub in Pea Croft for a drink. When they left there Maria met her husband outside her mother's and another quarrel ensued. At 10 o'clock the prisoner and his wife were having supper together in the Rawson's Arms in Fenton Street. He invited her to have some drink, and when she refused he said "You might as well have some while you have the chance; it will be the last time you have the chance".

They went home quietly together but in the middle of the night a scream was heard, and when a neighbour, Mrs. Kidnew, entered the prisoner's house she was met with a horrible sight. The body of Maria was on the floor in the kitchen. Her throat was cut and she was quite dead. The bodies of all the children were found on the floor in a bedroom upstairs. Their throats had been cut and they were all dead. The prisoner was also lying on the floor in the bedroom, and close by was a large table knife covered in blood and a candlestick. His throat was also cut. A man named Pearson said to him "Good God, what have you done?" He did not reply but put his hands to his lips as if praying. Later on he said "Let me lie, let me die". The prisoner was at once taken to the hospital and while being treated he said to the surgeon "Let me die" and "Cut my throat deeper". While in the hospital he thought he saw his children on the wall and asked them to go. When charged with murdering his wife and four children he said "It was all through drink; it was about midnight when I did it".

The five bodies were taken to the public mortuary on a corporation dray. Maria, apart from the gash to her throat, had sustained cuts and bruises to the face and to her wrists, suggesting that she had been beaten and restrained prior to death. All of the children had their throats cut, one so deeply that it was nearly decapitated. Another child's thumb was severed indicating that the child was trying to defend itself.

The only defence offered was that the prisoner was not at the time responsible for his acts. To support this it was described how until he was seven years old he suffered from brain fever for which he was treated by a doctor. His grandfather on his mother's side and his father were both found drowned and two brothers of his mother committed suicide, the one by cutting his throat, and the other by throwing himself under a train. The prisoner was subject to delusions. The surgeon at the Sheffiel hospital to which the prisoner was taken, Mr. St Clair White, gave evidence indicating that Laycock was not responsible for his acts at the time he committed the crimes. Nevertheless the jury found the prisoner guilty, and he was sentenced to death. At the point of death, Laycock exclaimed "Oh my children, my children. Lord have mercy on my children". The funerals were attended by 3,000 mourners.

James Murphy 1886

Murphy, from Barnsley, was a seasoned poacher with 25 convictions to his name. He was obviously unhappy about this unenviable record, wanted revenge and set out one day looking for a policeman called Austwick; when he found him he shot him dead. Murphy was duly arrested. This case demonstrates just how much public sympathy can be aroused for a convicted man and how powerful it can be: the popular feeling locally was that Murphy did not deserve to die. Nevertheless, Murphy's appeal failed and he was paid the usual visit in his cell by his hangman James Berry at which some gallows humour ensued when Murphy said 'I'm hanged if I can see what all the fuss is about'. Berry received threats before the execution and was advised never to set foot in Barnsley again because the Barnsley miners would murder him. He did set foot again in Barnsley, many times in fact. Murphy's name was forever linked to his reputation as a murderer after the publication of Charles Johnson's *Life of James Murphy – The Barnsley Murderer*.

James Richardson 1888

When James Richardson broke a brush at the brick-making factory where he worked in Barnsley he was admonished by his foreman, William Burridge, and sacked. Richardson stormed off, consumed with rage. But that was not the end of it; he sat waiting for Burridge to appear at the end of the shift – he had collected a gun from home – and blasted the foreman twice: once in the back, once in the head. Richardson initially fled but soon gave himself up and confessed. Burridge never woke from a coma and died in Leeds Beckett Hospital from 'disintegration and irritation of the brain'. Richardson was convicted to hang at Leeds Assizes despite the jury's recommendation for mercy. The only mitigation was that Burridge allegedly stuck his tongue out at Richardson when he came to pick up his wages, to humiliate him, and elbowed him in the stomach as he passed.

The two other criminals who were to hang alongside Richardson had their sentences commuted which gave him some hope. 7,000 people signed a petition to the Home Secretary pleading for clemency for Richardson; a number of the jurors wrote likewise; 3,000 locals attended a meeting proclaimed by the town crier protesting at the decision; a telegram was sent to Queen Victoria; a further meeting with 5,000 people attending was held; further telegrams were sent signed by the Mayor of Barnsley and other prominent officials – all to no avail.

The John Gill Slaughter 1889

Little John Gill was playing with friends near his home in Bradford; he never made it home. His body was found behind some stables – his limbs had been cut off and his heart ripped out; a piece of cloth from his coat tied round his neck. All of these atrocities were hallmarks of the Whitechapel ripper murders; indeed the Metropolitan Police had received a letter telling them 'I ripped up a little boy in Bradford'. Although a dairyman, on whose cart John was seen, was arrested, he was cleared.

Robert Kitching 1890

Kitching murdered Sergeant James Weedy because he was upset when the policemen asked him to move his horse and cart from outside the Leeming Bar Hotel. Kitching was heard to say that he would shoot Weedy, and then lay in wait for him; despite efforts by Kitching's wife to warn Weedy, the policeman was shot dead. Kitching pleaded self-defence but hanged at York.

Walter Turner 1891

On 10th June 1891 PC William Moss stumbled on a bundle in Alexander Street, Horsforth. The bundle was in fact the horribly mutilated body of five year old Barbara Whitham Waterhouse who had gone missing while playing outside her house. Her abdomen had been ripped open and her limbs almost severed, according to a local newspaper report. Ann Turner, mother of weaver Walter Lewis Turner, later told police that Walter had brought home 'an object' wrapped up in a cloth and concealed it in the coal cellar at their house, in Back Lane, Horsforth, telling his mother not to be concerned about it. Helped by his mother, he later took the body, wrapped in one of Ann Turner's shawls, to central Leeds in a tin trunk and dumped the corpse next to the police station in Horsforth, leaving the trunk on a railway station platform nearby. A dejected Ann Turner confided in a neighbour, Mary Cotterill, that a murder had been committed in her house. Mutilation of the body was extensive – Turner had stabbed Barbara 45 times and continued to butcher the body even after the child had died. She was covered in a white paste, established by the coroner, Mr. J.C. Malcolm, to be chloride of lime and applied by Turner's mother in a breathtaking show of unconditional devotion to her son. Not only did she thereby try to minimise the smell from the body but she also helped move the body.

Walter Turner was arrested and subsequently sentenced to death by hanging at Leeds Assizes in August 1891. Ann Turner was tried as an accessory but was acquitted, although some records say that she was jailed for a year as an accessory after the fact and others that she was jailed for life. The judge, Mr. Justice Grantham, in his closing speech suggested that had not Walter Turner been in police custody he would have been "torn limb from limb" by the locals. After passing sentence, Mr. Grantham presented the dead child's mother with a bouquet of flowers and received rapturous applause as he left the building.

Turner always maintained that he was innocent, claiming that he was drugged by a quarryman called Jack who left the body in his house while he was asleep.

James Stockwell 1892

When Mrs. Brooke, the landlady of the Ivy Bridge at Milnebridge, near Huddersfield, left her pub to go into town on the afternoon of 21st August she left her waitress, Catherine 'Kate' Dennis, a 16 year old Irish girl in charge of the bar. The solitary customer was Stockwell, sitting in the kitchen quietly eating a pie with a sharp knife. At 3p.m., John Iredale came in and stayed for 15 minutes; he did not see Stockwell and assumed he was the only person apart from the girl in the pub. On leaving, he passed two men on the way in. When a butcher's boy called on an errand an hour or so later he was unable to get in so called on a neighbour. They broke in and found Kate dead on the floor, a knife sticking from her neck. On learning of the murder, John Iredale contacted the police and told them about the two men he had seen going in the pub. They were soon apprehended and although one of them was carrying a knife, were found not to be implicated.

Mrs. Brooks returned and told the police about James Stockwell in the kitchen; they went to interview him but he had gone – in fact for several days he hid on the moors until he eventually gave himself up. At his trial at Leeds Assizes he claimed that the girl had pulled his hair as he lay sleeping and, angered by this, stabbed her in the neck with the knife. He was hanged in Armley Gaol.

Frederick Deeming 1892

Frederick Bailey Deeming (1853-1892) was an English-born Australian gasfitter, but he was much more famous as a murderer. He was convicted and executed for the murder of a woman in Melbourne, Australia and is remembered today as possibly being none other than Jack the Ripper. He murdered his first wife Marie, and his four children, at Rainhill, St. Helens, in July 1891, and a second wife, Emily Mather, at Windsor, Melbourne, on Christmas Eve 1891. He married his first wife, Marie James, in Tranmere in 1881 and lived for a short while in Birkenhead before leaving for Melbourne. By 1886 Deeming and Marie had two Australia-born daughters, Bertha and Marie. In 1888 he announced that he and his family were returning to England "with a considerable fortune".

His association with Yorkshire stems from the fact that it was to Hull that he returned and took lodgings in Beverley where he courted Helen Lydia Matheson, the 21 year old daughter of his landlady; he married her as Albert Williams, bigamously, in September 1891. After honeymooning in the south of England, he suddenly disappeared. In the meantime he gave the first Mrs. Deeming several hundred pounds telling her he was leaving for South America and would later send for her and the children. Before leaving he swindled a jeweller's in Hull and was arrested for this in Montevideo, extradited back to England on a charge of "obtaining goods by false pretenses" and was sentenced to nine months prison. On release Deeming stayed in a hotel in Rainhill and later moved into Dinham Villa where he complained that the drains were broken, and that a new kitchen floor was needed… eighteen months later the decomposed bodies of Marie Deeming and the four children – Bertha (aged ten), Mary (seven), Sidney (five) and Leala (eighteen months) – were found buried beneath the kitchen floor. In each case their throats had been cut, except Bertha who had been strangled.

In November 1891, Deeming sailed with Helen Matheson to Australia; they rented a house in Andrew Street, Windsor, a suburb of Melbourne. On 24th December or early on 25th December 1891, he murdered Mather and buried her under the hearthstone in one of the bedrooms, covering the body over with cement. Deeming left but on 3rd March 1892 a tenant complained of "a disagreeable smell" in the second bedroom. The owner and an estate agent lifted the hearthstone to investigate only to be met by a suffocating smell – "they found themselves barely able to breathe". The police found Mather's body and a postmortem revealed that Mathson's skull had been fractured by several blows, but that she had died from a cut throat.

Deeming was tried at Melbourne Supreme Court on 25th April 1892; a plea of insanity failed and he was sentenced to death. He was refused leave to appeal and on 19th May 1892 Deeming hanged.

John Gould 1893

John Gould lived with his father, 83 year old Henry in a caravan in Linthorpe, then a suburb of Middlesbrough; both were slaughtermen. Henry was concerned about his son's erratic behaviour and the fact that he had threatened someone with a muzzle loading shotgun. So, he reported the matter to a doctor, Dr. Scanlan, who visited John Gould on the pretext of getting him to put his horse down. Scanlan concluded that he was a lunatic. The doctor went back to Linthhorpe with a sanitary inspector and a policeman, only to be met by a frantic Henry Scanlan covered in blood and bruises caused during a scuffle trying to wrest a loaded gun from John. The three returned to the police station and later went back to the caravan with a PC Henderson – this time to be met with a gun-wielding John Gould and an unwelcoming mastiff dog. The dog was placated and the men split up: PC Henderson approached Gould but was shot and died instantly. Gould was overcome and taken into custody.

Henderson was 38 and left a widow and eight children, the youngest of whom were two year old twins. Police compensation was topped up by a public contribution. Gould, for his part, was detained in Northallerton gaol and at Leeds Assizes was found not guilty of murder due to insanity. He was committed to a lunatic asylum to be detained at her Majesty's Pleasure.

David Bell 1894

David Bell was a 55 year old steel worker at Samuelson & Co. in Newport, Middlesbrough. He had left his wife who had since died and for the past year lived with 50 year old Annie Burnett, mother of seven children; Bell and Annie lived with two of these children at 7 Old Buildings in Newport. One night he sought out a PC Davey in Newport Road to tell him that he had had an altercation with Annie and killed her. Although an alcoholic, Bell was a mild-mannered man and was sober this evening. Bell was charged; there was no weapon but there was blood on Bell's hands. The body was found on a mat in the living room with a knife wound to neck and a pool of blood; Annie had been sat sewing in a chair just before she was killed.

Bell was charged at Northallerton with murder with malice aforethought; he admitted murder but denied the malice, claiming that he had acted in a fit of passion. He explained that he was in the room paring his corns with a penknife; an argument erupted, Annie grabbed the knife and was fatally wounded. Medical experts refuted this pointing out that Annie had been stabbed more than once. Nelly, Annie's nine year old daughter testified that the couple had been sitting by the fire talking about getting married when Annie told Bell she did not want to. He called her a 'fucking Irish pig'; Nelly next heard a scream and went downstairs to find her mother dying.

Bell was convicted at York Assizes but with a strong recommendation for mercy; he won a reprieve and was given a life sentence of penal servitude instead.

The Death of Jane Smith 1894

Jane Smith, three and a half, lived with her parents in Cannon Street, Middlesbrough. Her father, William Smith, did something very unusual when he took out a policy on Jane's life. One night William and Mrs. Smith went out for a drink leaving Jane and another child of roughly the same age alone in the house with just a roaring fire to keep them company. Inevitably, Jane was severely burnt and died of her injuries.

The verdict was accidental death but with a request that the coroner reprimand the parents. This the coroner did, remarking on how unusual it was to insure a child so young and affirming that he would do everything he could to ensure that the Smiths received no insurance money.

George Stoner 1898

In 1898 George Stoner must have been one of the luckiest men alive because, against all odds, he lived to see 1899 – and much later after that.

'You'll be alright there Stoney' was the greeting Stoner got from a friend who saw him in Hull Docks with 37 year old Emily Hall, somewhat worse the wear for drink after drinking in the Theatre Tavern in Dock Street. Emily Hall was a prostitute who picked up George Stoner by Hull Docks, and together they checked in at 1 Princes Row, a cheap lodging house just off Dock Street, and behind the Queen's Dock. There, we know from medical reports at Hull Royal Infirmary, Stoner thrust a bar of soap deep into Hall's vagina which led to haemorrhaging and her death. Some reports say that he also stabbed her repeatedly in the genitals. When Stoner left without Emily Hall, the landlady, Elizabeth Shikovffsky, after some time went up to the room to check all was well. She found Hall bleeding profusely. Stoner was charged with her murder, but the jury returned a bizarre verdict: 'guilty of grievous bodily harm but without meditation'. The judge rejected this and Stoner was found guilty of murder, but a reprieve was issued on December 19th 1898 when the death sentence was commuted to penal servitude for life. By 1915 he was a free man and settled down to family life in Leeds.

Thomas Mellor 1900

Thomas Mellor hanged for drowning his two daughters, Ada Beecroft age six and Annie Beecroft age four in the Leeds-Liverpool Canal at Glebe Road, Holbeck, Leeds on Saturday, 11th May 1900. Actually, he was only convicted of the murder of Ada as no evidence was offered with regards to the murder of Annie.

Mellor was looking after the children on his own that day because their mother, who had been sent to Menston Asylum in Meanwood, had died in November 1899. Thomas Mellor had started co-habiting with another woman; they moved into lodgings in Fourth Court but were evicted; he then took the children to his brother's house, only to be told that they could not move in with him. He had also tried unsuccessfully to admit the children to the workhouse.

He told his brother's wife, when she asked him what he was going to do, that 'The water is big enough to hold them and me and all'. Thomas Mellor then took his children to the canal. He was seen walking with them around 11pm; around 11.30pm he was seen again, but without the girls. They were found drowned the next day in the canal. Mellor confessed to putting them in the canal but conceded that he had put them in a shallow part in the hope that someone would rescue them and take them into care.

Charles Blewitt 1900

Charles Blewitt, a tanner by trade, hanged at Leeds for the murder of his wife Mary Ann, the conviction being largely based on circumstantial evidence; no motive was ever established.

After ten days of inactivity at the Blewitts' home, Starfold in Beeston, Leeds, Charles' mother, naturally concerned, had the landlord, Thomas Armitage, force the door. Mary was found dead in her rocking chair with knife lacerations to her arms and neck; a shawl covered her neck wound. Defensive wounds on her wrists ruled out any suggestion of suicide. Strangely, Mary had asked her brother to look after her wedding certificate and a gun, to be returned at a later date. A thinly disguised Charles Blewitt, using the name Oliver Jackson, left Beeston for Halifax on the likely day of the murder; here a workmate at the Redman Foundry showed him a newspaper report of his wife's death, which also carried a picture of the wanted man – himself no less. Blewitt was quite unconcerned – a fact made much of by the prosecution at his trial: surely if he had been innocent of the crime, he would have been beside himself on discovering that his wife had died? He was turned in by colleagues, insisting all along that his wife must have committed suicide, a suggestion refuted by the attending physician who pointed out the defence wounds and the fact that there was no razor to be found near the body. If Mary Ann had slashed her own throat then the razor would have fallen to the floor. Crucially blood-spattered boots had been found at the scene, boots which belonged to Charles.

A sanguine Blewitt gave nothing away at the trial in Leeds which took two juries to reach a verdict.

The Murder of Anne Todd 1900

Cottingham today is a leafy suburb of Hull, on the way to Beverley and home to thousands of university students. In 1900 it was leafier still and the main street, Hallgate, was home to 78 year old widow, Anne Todd. Mrs. Todd was discovered by a neighbour lying in a pool of blood; she had been attacked with a poker and her house had been ransacked but, quite amazingly, she was still alive. Pots and pans were strewn all over but the money that she kept in the house was untouched. She later said that a man and a woman came to her door and the man said 'I'm going to do for you' to which she had replied 'You had better not'; the rest was a blank. Anne made a slow recovery, and was able to get about, walk up to ¾ of a mile; at first she continued to live in Cottingham but went to live with her brother-in-law, a cycle dealer, on Anlaby Road, on 23rd November 1900. She was taken ill on 5th December 1900 and died on 1st February 1901, so, within the year and a day specified by the law to define murder. That summer she had been 'in a semi-imbecile condition and was continually laughing'. Death was cerebral failure due to malnutrition because she could not take food, all of which was accelerated by her injuries. A verdict of wilful murder against some persons or person unknown was returned.

John Aaron Walker Jnr 1901

Twenty-one year old John Aaron Walker was convicted of the murder of his father, also called John Aaron Walker, and was sentenced to death but won a reprieve due to his age. He had stabbed his father in the chest killing him almost instantly in Raywell Street, Hull. Son and father had argued over alleged misconduct between John Walker and his step-mother. When the father had come downstairs threatening to destroy the house John Walker Jnr threw his father onto a chair and stabbed him in the heart with a knife saying that he always knew 'I would do for you'. John Walker Jnr's step-mother said that he had been living with them for four years or so although he had spent most of that time in prison.

John Walker Snr was a cellarman at the Grand Theatre in George Street, Hull; Charlotte Walker was a dresser there. Walker enjoyed a drink and when he drank whisky would often fly into a rage, smash up the furniture in their terrace in Jarratt's Place in Raywell Street; he would often smash up Charlotte Walker too. There was no love lost between father and son and one night in January 1901 this enmity exploded with a drunken father obscenely accusing Charlotte of being unfaithful to him with his son, her stepson. A fight ensued but Charlotte finally got Walker Snr to go back to bed; meanwhile, his son had taken a clasp knife from the drawer. The son attacked his father. Charlotte tried to staunch the massive blood loss and the son immediately regretted his action and begged forgiveness but his father soon died. He was charged at Norfolk Street Police Station with the murder of his father after which he was committed to trial at York Assizes. Here he was found guilty of murder with a strong recommendation for mercy on account of his relative youth and the provocation. He received a sentence of life imprisonment and the newly built gallows at Hull had to wait for their first victim.

The gallows at Hull were specially built for Walker but his reprieve meant that he missed out on the dubious privilege of being the first to hang there; previously Hull convictions hanged at York or Armley. In the event Arthur Richardson received the honour of christening the gallows when he was hanged by William Billington for the murder of Sarah Hebden, his aunt.

Arthur Richardson 1901

Richardson was convicted of the murder of his aunt, Sarah Hebden, aged 62, and sentenced to death. He had battered her to death at 97 Hodgson Street, Hull on Thursday 28th November 1901.

Sarah Hebden used to collect premium money for the Royal Liver Friendly Society for which she received a commission. She also had a tea caddy in which she generally kept between £5 and £10. Arthur Richardson had form for stealing from another aunt; he had only been released from prison eight days before he murdered Sarah Hebden. On 28th November 1901 Sarah Hebden failed to make a visit she had arranged to Elloughton; neighbours found a window open at the back of the house; they went in through the window and found Sarah dead at the foot of the stairs. Later, Arthur Richardson's landlord said that Richardson had complained to him that he had no money but then he saw him later with money in his pockets; Richardson later ordered a new suit and jacket and bought a gold albert.

When arrested, the police found a gold watch on him and a brooch that belonged to Sarah Hebden and they found bloodstains on his clothes and boots. Richardson was found guilty of murder and hanged at Hull Prison.

Emily Swann & John Gallagher – the Wombwell Murder 1903

When 30 year old John Gallagher, a glass blower, started lodging in the Wombwell home of Emily Swann and William Swann it seems he wasted no time in starting a relationship with the 42 year old mother of eleven. Neighbours reported that William was frequently abusive to his wife – suspicion about an affair cannot have helped. Nevertheless, Gallagher resolved to move out and relocate to Bradford – but before he did, in June 1903, Emily turned up at a neighbour's house sporting two black eyes and facial bruising. As it happened, Gallagher was at the neighbour's and when he saw her injuries, flew into a rage and shouted, "I'll go and give him something for himself for that… I'll coffin him before morning." The sound of fighting went on for ten minutes or so, after which Gallagher emerged and went back to the neighbour's house where he exclaimed "I've busted four of his ribs and I'll bust four more. I'll finish him out before I go to Bradford." Returning to the Swanns' house, he said, "I'll murder the pig before morning. If he can't kick a man he shan't kick a woman." The fighting resumed; a neighbour heard Emily say, "Give it to him, Johnny."

Johnny obviously did 'give it to him', for, ten minutes later Emily and John came out holding hands and, according to nieghbours, showing "every sign of affection." William Gallagher was dead. When the police arrived, they arrested Emily but Gallagher escaped and was on the run for two months, sleeping rough, before he was apprehended at a relative's' house in Middlesbrough.

At the trial in October 1903 at Leeds Assizes Gallagher's threat to "finish him out before I go to Bradford" was adjudged as intent. "As for the woman" said the judge, "it is my duty to tell you that one does not commit murder only with one's hands. If one person instigates another to commit murder, and that other person does it, the instigator is also guilty of murder." This is an example of Common Purpose where the law states that if two or more people commit a crime, they can be held equally responsible where there was common purpose: they both intended, or could have reasonably foreseen, the outcome.

Both were found guilty; when asked if she had anything to say before the death sentence was passed, a calm Emily asserted, "I am innocent." "I am not afraid of immediate death, because I am innocent and will go to God." Emily Swann and Gallagher were then formally sentenced to death by hanging. Emily remained sanguine: after she was sentenced she smiled and blew a kiss to someone in the gallery as she was taken down.

Some evidence had been withheld and not put before the jury because it was deemed prejudicial to Emily's case. The judge informed the jury that when Gallagher was taken into custody, he had alleged that Emily struck William with a poker, and that he did not touch the dead man, although he was obviously present at the scene of the crime.

The pair were held in Armley Gaol and advised that 29th of December was the date of their executions. Both allegedly ate a hearty Christmas dinner. Double (and treble hangings) were still permitted in 1903 so Emily and Gallagher were executed side by side. Just before 8 o'clock, Emily Swann was in a terrible state groaning on the floor of her cell but, after a drink of brandy, she pulled herself together and walked to the execution room where she greeted the hooded and pinioned Gallagher with , "Good morning John"; although stunned by her presence, he replied "Good morning love." The noose was placed round her neck; her final words were "Good-bye. God bless you."

James Henry Clarkson 1903

James Henry Clarkson murdered 12 year old Elizabeth Mary Lynas in a yard at 9 Bennison Street, Guisborough, on 27th December 1903 while she was returning from church. She was found in nearby woods: her throat had been cut and her legs and hands had been bound. Clarkson lived with his wife and sister but could not provide an alibi, falsely claiming that he was drinking in the Applegarth pub at the time: a bloodstained razor, Elizabeth's tam o'shanter and bloody clothes were found in the house, and he was charged with murder. Clarkson hanged at Armley Gaol; it was later revealed that he always fainted at the sight of blood.

John Thomas Kay 1904

John Thomas Kay was yet another victim of drink, or rather his already married common law wife was when Kay slew her with a hatchet in Rotherham in 1904. Kay confessed immediately; when the police arrived at the scene of the crime, the victim, Jane Hirst, was still alive although she died soon after. Before the murder there was a history of violence and drink in the short-lived relationship including the time when Kay, drunk, threw Hirst out of the house for alleged infidelity. Indeed, he claimed he was so drunk on the day of the murder that he had no idea what he was doing. The mitigation cut no ice and Kay was hanged at Armley.

George Smith 1905

In June 1905 Martha Smith was working as a domestic servant for a Mr. Shelton in Burley Road, Leeds. Her husband, George, was idle and a wastrel; Mr. Shelton, out of consideration for Martha, rebuked him for this. Martha then left Leeds, left her job and left her husband, and took up a post in Ilkley in Riddings Road. George followed her, went to the house and stabbed her in a frenzy 40 times, leaving her in a pool of blood. Smith was arrested in Wakefield, asserting that he just happened to have a penknife on him and that he had no recollection of the attack. George Smith was hanged.

Thomas Tattersall 1905

When Thomas Tattersall, plasterer, was busy plastering the execution cell at Wakefield Prison, he could not have known that he would be soon looking at the inside of another execution cell – this time at Armley Gaol with the significant difference that the door here would be locked behind him. Tattersall was a drunk; moreover, he had a reputation for beating Rebecca, his wife, and, although the house was under surveillance by the police, cut her throat with a razor and cleaved her skull with an axe in July 1905. When Laura, their daughter, went to help he threatened to murder her but she it was who told neighbours what had happened. His excutioner, John Billington, died two months later as a result of a fall he had taken while getting ready for Tattersall's hanging.

Harry Walters 1906

Harry Walters is remarkable because he was only one of ten killers hanged at Wakefield; but he is also notable because he committed one of the most depraved murders ever recorded in Yorkshire. Sarah McConnell, 43, had left her husband and now lived in lodgings with Walters in Allen Street, Sheffield; two days before Christmas 1906 her half-naked bleeding body was discovered by her landlady, Elizabeth Drakard. A beer bottle had been thrust into her vagina, and then a broom handle, apparently up to her neck. Walters was seen by a little girl stooped over McConnel, pretending to help her… a woman by the name of Revill later said that she heard Walters say that he would kill Sarah 'as soon as we are alone' and that he would kill her if she did not find him money. He was convicted of wilful murder at Wakefield.

John Ellwood 1908

Nothing can get anywhere close to the anguish and anxiety evoked by waiting for the decision of an Appeal Court as to whether you hang or you live. When John Ellwood killed Thomas Wilkinson he, like many others, had to go through just that. Employee-employer relations were at the heart of the case: Ellwood had been fired, after a row, by Fieldhouse & Jowett in Swain Street, Leeds. One morning he bought a poker for the specific purpose of killing Thomas Wilkinson and settling a grudge, and robbing the firm. Ellwood turned up unannounced and uninvited one Friday, payday, on the pretext that he was there for a meeting to get his job back. Blood was found on his clothing which he ascribed to a nosebleed. The appeal against hanging for murder arose from the failure of a defence witness to show at the trial. The appeal was refused and Ellwood hanged at Armley Gaol.

Thomas Siddle 1908

Gertrude Siddle, 22, had had enough of her lazy and feckless husband, 29 year old bricklayer Thomas, so she upped sticks and moved to Hull with the two children, lodging in the house of Mrs. Mabel Felcey at Strathfield House in Tyne Street. The children were Harry, fourteen months and Ethel, three. As Siddle failed to make adequate provision for Gertrude and her children, she obtained a separation order, and then a commitment order for maintenance against him. This was when Thomas called at her lodgings about five weeks later, ostensibly to say goodbye before going to prison because he could not pay, or, as he euphemistically put it, 'going down the road for the non-payment of the order'.

But he had noticed a ring on her finger which she had not got from him; unusually, he had probably not had a drink. He had, though, come equipped with a razor. Assuming she was having an affair, Thomas slashed his wife's throat while holding one of the children. Despite her serious wound Gertrude dashed to a chemist and was taken to hospital where she died. When the police arrived, Thomas Siddle was still sitting where he was when he attacked Gertrude; his defence that he had been drinking for nine weeks and had eaten nothing, and had acted out of provocation and impulse, fell on deaf ears and he was hanged at Hull. The children ended up in Beverley Road workhouse. The ring was explained by Mabel Felcey who told the court that Gertrude had pawned her own for 1/6d and that she had given her one of hers as a replacement.

John Freeman 1909

When it comes to male murderers, the explosive combination of drink and women can form a terrible catalyst. This was the case with John and Robert Freeman who lived together with Florence, Robert's wife in Hull's Porter Street. After a heavy night in the Myton Tavern Robert accused his brother of having an affair with Florence, also drunk by this time. The inevitable fight ensued in which John stabbed Florence fatally in the neck. Concerned neighbours witnessed this, and the ongoing fight. John was arrested and sentenced to death. Robert forgave John.

The Death of Maud Waines' Baby 1909

Bridlington was the setting of the death of Maud Waines' baby when it was found wrapped in linen in a parcel by a man called Stubbs on Sands Lane railway bridge. The 23 year old mother found herself in the dock as a result. The linen was traced back to Maud. A search of her rooms revealed a bottle of apiolene – prescribed to induce miscarriage – and a doctor certified that the baby was not stillborn and a wound was observed on its skull, which could have occurred during birth. Nevertheless, Maud was in the dock charged with wilful murder.

The case was repeatedly ajourned due to Maud's fragile health but when it was heard, it emerged that she had had a rash liaison with a Mr. Foster who worked at the British Oil Mill Company in Hull and was the father of the baby; having seduced her he then disappeared. The court heard that the baby had died from a fall and that in her distress Maud had held on to the baby. She was of good character, a loving mother for the little time she was one and suffered alone and in silence from the stigma and shame associated with her pregnancy out of wedlock, not telling her parents who lived in Burton Agnes. The charge was commuted to concealment of birth at York Assizes. Maud had given birth while unconscious and the baby had fallen. She was bound over with a £5 fine.

Charles Brown 1910

An enjoyable day at Beverley races was on the cards for Walter Henry Nozedar and his nephews Walter Edward and James William – from Raywell Street in Hull. What was not on the cards were three tarted up prostitutes from Hull, behaving indecorously to say the least. They hurled obscenities at the three

Nozedars as they passed by to which Edward responded: he confronted one of the women who threatened him with her hairpin. A crowd had soon formed from which a heavily-built man emerged demanding to know what the trouble was. This was Charles Brown who thumped Edward to the ground and did likewise to Walter when he came to help. One of the prostitutes kicked Walter as he lay on the ground. James too was felled before Brown threatened a charity collector from Hull Children's Hospital and stormed off to the beer tent. When police arrived they examined Edward Nozedar believing that he may well be dead; Brown had left with the three women in a wagonette. The police gave chase, Brown threatened the driver with a hammer but was finally arrested and charged with assault; the women were charged with riotous behaviour and all three spent the night in the cells. A doctor from Newbegin, Beverley later pronounced Edward dead and Brown was charged with feloniously killing and slaying Walter Edward Nozedar, a charge he refuted blaming the death on the kicking administered by the women.

Brown, from Leeds, a bookie's helper, was tried at York Assizes for manslaughter. Edward had died from a heart attack due to violent blows; Brown was found guilty. His inglorious record was read out in court: 28 convictions in Leeds courts in his 28 years. Five years penal servitude is what he got in addition to the balance of a sentence he was already serving as a ticket of leave man. Two of the women went to jail for riotous behaviour.

George Lumb 1911

George Lumb had mental issues and personality disorders as a result of a serious childhood accident; he lived in a shared house in Castleford. His mother, Jane, was sick, he was unemployed and probably unemployable, and the family doctor, Saville Bentley, had unhelpfully signed away his rights to benefits. When Bentley next made a house call to treat his mother, Lumb was waiting for him with a loaded gun: Lumb shot Bentley in the chest. Despite his injury, Bentley returned to his trap and ordered the groom to get him to Leeds Infirmary as quickly as possible. Once there a lengthy operation saved his life.

Meanwhile the police had arrived at Lumb's house, concerned about the safety of Jane Lumb. Negotiations were to no avail when Lumb, in response to questions about her, said 'Oh, she's alright; I've made short work of her. She's ready for the box'. At this an Inspector Fred Stafford leapt up the stairs under fire from Lumb, holding a metal sheet to defend himself and arrested Lumb. Lumb had shot his mother in the head and tried to argue that his mother had put the gun in her mouth and pulled the trigger, instructing him to finish her off; Lumb alleged that his is exactly what he did. Forensics showed, however, that she died from a single shot to the temple. Oddly, no plea for insanity was offered and Lumb was convicted of murder at Leeds Assizes. He did not help his own cause by not allowing his counsel to conduct a proper defence. However, an appeal led the Home Secretary, taking note of the mental issues, to commute the death sentence to life imprisonment.

George Law 1913

George Frederick Law, a Sheffield engineer, murdered his landlady Annie Cotterill by strangling her and slashing her face. All had been well until Law, a lodger with the Cotterills for two and a half years, was given notice to leave – news which infuriated him. James Cotterill was so worried by the threats Law made against them that he removed all razors from the house. On October 21st 1913, Law left for work but returned to the lodgings where Annie Cotterill lay in bed ill. When James, her husband, returned to the house he had to force entry through a window; it was then that he discovered the body of his wife. Law was found in Nottinghamshire and, despite efforts to convince that he was insane, hanged at Wakefield.

John McCartney 1915

When Charlotte Kent checked into lodgings in Pocklington as Charlotte MacDonald she could have had no idea where it was all going to end. As it happened, John William McCartney, real name Harry MacDonald, an army cook in a town awash with soldiers, had married a woman Hilda even though he was already married to Bridget Whyles. He was 39, Charlotte was 28. But McCartney was a violent and abusive man who almost strangled Hilda on a number of occasions and threatened 'to do her in one of these days'. He had accused her of having an affair with a Cpl. Buxton. Charlotte's landlady, Eliza Walker refused to let McCartney stay at her lodgings in future. But the violence continued with Charlotte sometimes giving as good as she got. When she refused to spend the night with him on the camp he cut her throat with a razor. After trial and sentencing in York, he claimed insanity but was convicted of murder; he was transferred to Wakefield – the last prisoner to hang there.

Willam Burkitt 1915-1935

Burkitt was one of nine children, a Hull fisherman with a conviction for desertion in the First World War. He was a very lucky man – a triple murderer with Lady Luck on his side. Not so his three unfortunate victims. He stabbed married woman Mary Jane (Polly) Tyler in 1915 in a row over a photograph; he then gave Polly's son the keys to the murder house in Hull and told him to give it the first policemen he saw: 'there you will find your mother dead'. Burkitt got manslaughter at York with twelve year's hard labour. The judge was less than impressed with his excuse that Mary Tyler kept nagging him…

In 1924 he started living with Helen Spencer and when he returned from a spell at sea stabbed her in the throat for allegedly being unfaithful. The police arrived to find that he had tried to gas himself; insanity was the plea and this time he served ten years, again for manslaughter. He told the court that she had startled him when waking him up and he had lashed out, not realising it was Helen … When he came out of Dartmoor, the 'Iron Man' murdered Emma Brookes and was sentenced to penal servitude for life at Leeds.

On 1st March 1935, Burkitt had turned up at his sister's house foaming at the mouth: he said that he had taken 600 aspirins. The tablets appeared not to be working so he left and jumped into the River Humber. He was rescued and taken to hospital. When police went to check his home, they found the body of Mrs. Brookes, who had been strangled. In 1954, he was released as an act of mercy, and was admitted to Hull Infirmary; he disappeared in 1955 but was caught soon after. He died of cancer on 24th December 1956.

The West Hull Mystery 1917

When Private Fred Dry went to a Hull police station to report the death of his wife in Chanterlands Avenue, he was naturally a suspect. Fred Dry had found his wife in bed, her skull smashed and stab wounds to her chest. Before he had left to fight in France the marriage had been somewhat tempestuous: he was a flirt and had written letters to various other women. Dry confessed to uxoricide, was sentenced to hang, with a recommendation to mercy.

When Dry had returned from France he was hospitalised and later found that his wife was virtually cohabiting with a man called Spooner. Dry may have been suffering from post-traumatic stress disorder but what was beyond any doubt was that his father had died in an alysum and his sister was currently committed to a mental institution. No defence of insanity was offered at the trial. A date was fixed for the execution; a petition to the Home Secretary was lodged; the sentence was commuted to penal servitude for life.

Robert Gadsby 1918

When Robert Gadsby murdered his girlfriend Julia Ann Johnson aged 54, whose throat he cut at 3 Thrift Crescent, Waterloo Lane, Bramley on 28th February 1917, it was not the murder that was particularly notable, but rather his Quixotic behaviour during the trial. He confessed the crime to the police but made the mistake of telling them that he grew angry when she abused him and showed him the door; he drew his penknife and killed her. In a court of law this was indicative of an intention to inflict grievous bodily harm or to kill.

So, Gadsby changed his story and claimed that Julia Johnson attacked him while he was shaving and attempted to slash his throat; she died in the ensuing struggle. No one believed this fiction and Gadsby was hanged at Leeds for wilful murder.

Annie Neath 1917 and 1921

Annie Elizabeth Neath was a single woman in domestic service at the Junction Inn in Leeds Road, Bradford. She called a doctor when she apparently felt ill and told him that her baby had been born prematurely and was under the bed – with scissor stab wounds which she said were caused accidentally. Annie was acquitted of a murder charge but served eighteen months without hard labour for manslaughter.

Annie Neath struck again in Halifax four years later in very similar circumstances and with a near identical *modus operandi*. She was in service for a George and Elizabeth Hinchliffe in Rhodesia Road (no doubt unaware of her previous conviction) where she concealed another pregnancy from her employer and secretly delivered the infant, a seven-pound boy, alone in her room. Then she stabbed him to death with scissors and went downstairs to start her working day, but complaining of feeling dizzy. Elizabeth Hinchliffe noticed bloodstains on the bed which Annie explained away by saying that she had vomited blood. After numerous examinations by a doctor and a nurse Annie was admitted to hospital for an operation: both doctor and nurse had noticed physiological abnormalities. It was while Annie was in hospital that the baby was found under her bed in a basket with fifteen puncture wounds, one of which punctured the heart and would have been the cause of death. Two more punctured the brain, one the throat as far as the vertebrae and the others the lungs and liver. Bloodied scissors and a copy of the *Midwives Pronouncing Dictionary* were found with two pages folded back.

The defence presented no evidence but the judge said that she probably did it subconsciously as a result of the pain she was in when she collapsed. Neath, eighteen, was sentenced to hang but reprieved, like many other women who killed. She contracted tuberculosis while in prison and died from it in 1932.

Sarah Ann Woodhead 1918

Sarah Ann Woodhead was a soldier's wife from Wibsey near Bradford; she was convicted of the manslaughter of her newborn by throwing it on the fire and received a sentence of fifteen months.

Edwin Sowerby 1920

Like schizophrenia, post traumatic stress disorder in the 1920s was barely recognised as a medical condition, never mind as a defence in law. Mutism, paralysis and exhaustion, for example, were ascribed to changes in atmospheric pressure rather than the sheer terror of being bombarded or sniped at day and night. When Edwin Sowerby, 26 and a miner, returned from the front in 1918 to his home in North's Yard in Crofton and was demobbed, he exhibited clear signs of having been seriously traumatised by his experiences in the trenches. Head pains and suicidal thoughts pointed to only one diagnosis.

When his 19 year old girlfriend, Jane or Janie Darwell, ended their relationship in 1920 Edwin dealt with it by approaching her at a cricket club dance at Crofton near Wakefield and cutting her throat, in full view of all around. Edwin failed in his attempt to cut his own throat with the razor and was rushed to the Clayton Hospital in Wakefield. Jane had worked for a while at the Barnbow Munitions Factory in Leeds during the war. This was seen as a clear case of wilful murder with no mitigating circumstances; he hanged at Leeds.

Lee Doon 1922

Thirty-three year old Sing Lee owned a chain of laundries and lived over the shop at 231 Crookes Road, Sheffield. Also living there was 27 year old Lee Doon, a Chinese laundry worker who had recently come from Liverpool to work in Sing Lee's laundry. Another of Sing Lee's employees was Lily Siddall: at the end of play on Saturday 9th September 1922, Sing Lee asked her if she could put in a shift the following morning. Lily agreed; it was something of a surprise for her to be told by Doon on Sunday morning that Sing Lee "Go back China. Business belong me."

Lily was suspicious: Lee Doon was wearing Sing Lee's trousers and Lily, seeing Sing's trilby on the hat stand and his attaché case, asked Lee Doon why he had not taken them with him when he left; Doon was clearly lying when he said that he gone to town on the Saturday night and bought new ones. She became even more suspicious when Doon got two workers in to dig a hole in the cellar floor. She later saw Doon struggling to move a heavy trunk and became frantic when a female friend of Sing Lee's came to the laundry to find out why Lee had stood her up the previous evening. She made some fruitless enquiries including a trip to Liverpool to talk to Sing Lee's relatives, and eventually called the police who came to the laundry around midnight on the following Friday. They found Sing Lee's body concealed in a tin trunk, 'trussed up like a fowl', covered with just a shirt, and buried in the hole in the cellar under tons of coal and coke.

Lee Doon claimed that he had fought with Sing Lee over the morphine he was taking: Sing Lee had allegedly suggested smoking opium or taking morphine. Sing Lee had insulted him and in the ensuing brawl Sing Lee fell, hit his head on the stove and died. Fear of the consequences led Lee Doon to hide the body. But at the trial it was revealed that there were no traces of morphia in his body. The trunk also contained bloodstained bedding and a post mortem revealed that Sing Lee had sustained severe and gaping wounds to the head and extensive fractures to the skull from a blunt instrument. A rope had been fastened tightly around his neck. A further investigation revealed bloodstains in Lee's bedroom: the police surgeon concluded that Sing Lee had been attacked whilst asleep in bed and that his body had been moved to the cellar after death.

Doon Lee got murder; a plea for manslaughter failed, as did his request to be beheaded rather than hanged. He was hanged at Armley Gaol. Lily Siddall deserves the highest commendation for her detective work and persistence; she went to extraordinary lengths to find out what actually happened on that night and was not prepared to believe the lies peddled by Lee Doon. Some of the local papers called her a "modern day Miss Marple".

John Eastwood 1923

When John Eastwood got it into his head that John Clark was getting over familiar with his wife he took the law and a hatchet into his hands and went calling at Clark's house. Eastwood had recently run away to Liverpool with his mistress, Mildred, but had second thoughts and returned to Walkley in Sheffield to resume normal life with his wife at the Bay Horse, the pub they ran together. But Mrs. Eastwood evidently had other plans so Eastwood resorted to the pub hatchet. When Clark opened his front door, Eastwood smashed him on the head. Eastwood confessed and tried to persuade the court that he committed the crime out of insanity – indeed, to support his case he could prove that he had recently been admitted to Eccleshall Institute with syphilis. The plea failed and Eastwood was hanged.

Grace Castle 1923

Grace Castle of Driffield murdered her three children; the servant, Alice Harper, discovered her one night in the bathroom with her drowned children. 'Oh my poor bairns' she said and explained 'I've done it for the best because my sins were great'. Wilful murder was never going to stick; the judge found her unfit to plead and sentenced her to Broadmoor. Postpartum psychosis or puerperal psychosis – a severe episode of mental illness which begins suddenly in the days following childbirth was not widely recognised in 1923. This judge, however, was circumspect enough to realise that Grace's depressive episode was a mitigating factor.

Symptoms vary and can quickly fluctuate . They include high mood (mania), depression, confusion, hallucinations and delusions. Postpartum psychosis is a psychiatric emergency. It is much less common than baby blues or postnatal depression. It occurs in about 1 in every 1,000 women (0.1%) who have a baby.

Hubert Dalton 1924

Some murders are inexplicable: why, for example, would Hubert Dalton want to murder most savagely, his life-long best friend 68 year old Francis Ward? Frank Ward had worked as a railway bank man on the Rosedale line for 40 years and lived at the foot of the slope in Bank Foot Cottage in Ingelby Greenhow near Great Ayton. He was going on holiday to Whitby the following day. Dalton was a railway platelayer; he lived near to Ward at Poultry House Crossing and usually spent Friday evenings drinking and playing dominoes in the Dudley Arms with Ward. On Friday evening, 3rd October, 1924, the men were met by their boss Edward Carpenter, who gave them their weekly pay packets. Ward opened his and checked the contents – two pounds nine shillings and sixpence – and put the money in a small purse in his back pocket. After his tea, Ward set off for Ingleby Greenhow three miles away with a canvas bag containing his life savings of about one hundred pounds. However, Ward failed to show at the pub that evening; his daughter, beside herself with worry waited all night for him to return. Next morning, Edward Carpenter called the police who found Frank Ward's body near a haystack in a pool of blood. His skull had been crushed and his throat cut and his money and two watches were missing. A search of the Daltons' outhouse discovered Ward's purse containing eleven pounds ten shillings and a railway ticket made out to Frank Ward to Whitby. A sack containing a bloodstained hammer was also recovered.

During the search Dalton came staggering towards the police from the nearby railway line with a self-inflicted throat wound to give the impression that he too had been a victim. Great Ayton doctor Dr. Robert Murray stitched up Dalton's wound and admitted him to North Ormesby Hospital. Dalton was charged with murdering Frank Ward; the committal proceedings were held in Stokesley Town Hall where the room was brightly decorated in preparation for a new year's eve ball. He was tried at York Assizes in spring 1925 and pleaded insanity; the jury failed to reach a verdict. The prosecution claimed robbery as the motive; death was caused by hammer blows from a hammer which had been found nearby. It was also alleged that Dalton had returned to the body in the early hours, and by candle light had cut Ward's throat to ensure he was dead. The case was reconvened at Leeds Assizes before the same judge. As before, the defence was insanity; Dalton was sentenced to death. An appeal failed and he was hanged at Hull on 10th June 1925.

William Wardell 1924

Sixty-year old Elizabeth Reaney was looking forward to starting a new life in Derby, moving there from her home in Sunderland Road, Manningham, Bradford which she had sold vacant possession. There was a quantity of banknotes in her house on February 23rd 1924. She had a visitor who battered her to death with a coal hammer. Bogus letters from a non-existent Mr. Goodson were found at Sunderland Road; a local at the Peel Hotel where Wardell drank said he walked with Wardell near to the house. Banknotes belonging to Elizabeth Reaney and the letters were traced back to Wardell; he was hanged at Armley Gaol.

Louie Calvert 1925

When 33 year old Louie Calvert was confronted by her landlady, Mrs. Lily Waterhouse, over the theft of bits and pieces from her boarding house and reported her to the police she battered and strangled her to death. Just before her execution she admitted to the murder of a previous employer, John Frobisher, in 1922. Louie Calvert was hanged at Strangeways on 24th June 1926, the first woman to be executed at the prison since 1886. Her execution attracted a crowd outside the prison gates of some 500 people, mostly women, who lingered until the death notice was displayed on the prison gates.

Louie Calvert was bad-tempered, a petty thief and prostitute known to the police as Louie Gomersal and as Louie Jackson to the Salvation Army – she was a member of their congregation; she had two illegitimate children; in 1925, she worked as a housekeeper for Albert Calvert, a night watchman living at 7 Railway Place in the Pottery Fields area of Leeds. After working for him for two or three months she told him she was pregnant. Calvert immediately married her.

As time went by, Albert Calvert could not fail to wonder when their baby was going to arrive. Louie responded by telling him that she was going to stay with her sister in Dewsbury to have the baby. When she got to Dewsbury she sent her unsuspecting husband a telegram to confirm her safe arrival and then returned to Leeds where she took up lodgings with the eccentric 40 year old widow Mrs. Lily Waterhouse in Amberley Road. Lily attended séances and attracted numerous men to her house. Louie had agreed to act as maid to pay for her board but she did no work and started to pawn Mrs. Waterhouse's silverware instead. This was when Lily went to the police and filed a complaint.

As it happened, a teenage girl with an unwanted baby daughter agreed to let Louie adopt her child; the day after Mrs. Waterhouse had been to the police, neighbours heard a loud banging from her house. Louie left the house with the baby explaining the commotion to the concerned neighbours by saying that the baby's bed had collapsed. A Mrs. Clayton said to Louie that she thought she had heard what she thought was Mrs. Waterhouse making strange noises. Louie confirmed this, saying 'I have left her in bed crying because I am leaving her.'

When a policeman visited the house to find out why Mrs. Waterhouse had not pursued her complaint, he got wind of the noises, obtained a key and found Mrs. Waterhouse battered and strangled to death on the bed. She was bare-footed. When police arrested Louie they found her wearing Lily's boots despite the fact that they were too large; some of the missing property was also found there.

The police soon linked Louie with the death four years earlier of a man named John Frobisher with whom she had been involved at Mercy Street, Wellington Lane, Leeds. His body had been found by a policeman on 12th of July 1922, floating in the Leeds-Liverpool Canal with a wound on the back of his head and a fractured skull. Significantly, Frobisher was discovered without his boots on though otherwise fully dressed. So, in two completely unrelated cases of murder Louie had stolen her victim's boots even though they were a bad fit.

At Leeds Assizes Louie claimed that she was pregnant and could not, therefore, be hanged until after she had given birth. An examination found that she might be in the early stages of pregnancy but that it would not prevent her from being hanged. This caused considerable public concern and a petition for a reprieve was signed by two to three thousand people, many from her home town of Ossett. The reprieve was rejected and the post mortem confirmed it to be a fabrication.

Alfred Bostock 1925

Alfred Bostock and Elizabeth Sherratt both worked for the Parkgate Ironworks in Rotherham: it was love at first sight and even though Bostock was married it did not deter him from having a passionate affair with Elizabeth. Things were fine until Elizabeth told Bostock that she was pregnant; this was not part of his plan. On May 3rd 1925, Elizabeth's battered body was found floating in the river at Rawmarsh. Bostock was the prime suspect and was soon arrested for the murder. Even though the evidence against him was largely circumstantial, it took the jury a mere 15 minutes to convict him. Bostock was one half of a double hanging at Armley; he shared the scaffold with 23 year old Wilfred Fowler.

Wilfred and Lawrence Fowler 1925

Wilfred Fowler was a Sheffield gangster who was involved in the murder of an ex-boxer called William Plommer who was ambushed in the street by the Fowlers. Fowler's brother and leader of the gang, Lawrence, was to hang the following day for the same crime. The gang were terrorising the city and, as is often the case, saw themselves as being above the law. One of the gangsters, Trimmer Welsh, had ill advisedly got into a fight with William Plommer over the way he was treating the barmaid in the pub where they were drinking; predictably Plommer came out easily on top. Plommer was then waylaid by two other members of the gang, including Wilfred Fowler; they too took a beating. Enough was enough, so a dozen of the gang went to Plommer's house where they beat, stabbed and kicked him to death. The mob members were soon rounded up: some received prison sentences while Lawrence and Wilfred Fowler were convicted of murder and sentenced to hang. Their deaths signalled an end to the gang rule in Sheffield in the 1920s.

Catherine Thorpe 1925

When Douglas Hodgkins passed a man and woman arguing in a Bradford street she heard the woman promise that she would 'not be humbugged by him any more'. Nothing unusual there but then she produced a butcher's knife from her handbag, stabbed him in the chest, panicked and called for an ambulance. She screamed, 'If I have done it, it is because I love him'. Her victim was a musician, Herbert Musgrave, her 23 year old husband; she, Kitty, was 26, separated from her husband and was struggling to find work. She met Herbert in the Grosvenor Hotel. He later promised they would set up home together and borrowed money from her which he, to Kitty's irritation, would not repay.

Wilful murder was the verdict since the judge could see no sudden passion in the attack. The trial was held at Leeds Assizes where friends had had a whip round to pay for a good barrister. To no avail, she pleaded not guilty: the jury returned a guilty verdict 'but under great provocation' and recommended mercy. The judge was having none of it and donned his black cap; Kitty collapsed on hearing the verdict. An appeal to commute the sentence to manslaughter was held. The good news was that there was considerable moral judgement relating to Musgrave's lifstyle: he was a pub piano player, had two children but had left his wife. The bad news was that Kitty had said the day before the attack that she was going 'to do someone in'. The manslaughter issue was soon rejected as was the question of provocation: the judges did, however, offer mercy and Kitty Thorpe was sentenced to penal servitude for life.

Samuel Case 1927

When steelworker George Mottram finished his shift he returned to his home in Ravencarr Road, Leeds as usual. However, he could never have expected the sight which awaited him in the unusually unlit house. His wife lay dead on the floor strangled by a clothes line, her face swollen, her glasses broken and her purse missing. Her murderer, Samuel Case, had known Mrs. Mottram since school and confessed to the murder. However, things were not be so straightforward because a man called Walter Hartle also confessed to the murder: he had walked to Leeds with Case and alleged that he hid in a cupboard and leapt out on Mrs. Mottram. All utter nonsense. Case hanged at Armley Gaol.

Mary Jane Learoyd 1929

The naked body of Mary Learoyd, a 36 year old clerk, was found on wasteland at Sedbergh Park in Ilkley, but her murderer never was found, despite witness sightings of a courting couple in the area at about the time of Mary's death. She was a friendly, sociable girl with many friends, good looking and happy to talk to anyone she met. One witness, Alice Kears who lived nearby, heard a voice say 'Wait a minute and I'll kiss you', followed by a scream. Mary's torn clothes were scattered around her body; she had been beaten to death. There were unhelpful rumours about her having an affair with a married clergyman.

Mary Jane's murder was particularly sordid. A stocking was tied around her neck; another was used to tie her hands. One nipple was smeared with mud, a broken comb had been inserted in her vagina and a metal cigarette case in her rectum, both after death. Someone with bloodstained fingers had wiped them on her body; a vaginal contraceptive ring was found at the scene, amongst other items.

Arthur Raveney 1929

Private Arthur Leslie Raveney was arrested on the Great North Road on 14th May 1929 and held at Bedale Police Station before being escorted back to Catterick Camp; he was absent without leave having been confined to barracks for a minor offence and was guarded by a Private Leslie Gordon White. Raveney could boast an exemplary record in the Royal Tank Corps so his behaviour was puzzling. What the (unarmed) arresting sergeants failed to discover in their search was the gun Raveney had presumably concealed: at Constable Burton Raveney used this gun to shoot Private White in the Land Rover and then fled to Finghall and then to a quarry in Newton-le-Willows. The sergeants sped off to get medical help for Private White who was still alive at this stage.

A Constable Cartwright borrowed a horse from some gypsies and pursued Raveney to the quarry where he was now trapped. The only problem was that the fugitive was armed despite the earlier search. The answer to how he got the gun was that Raveney had a weapon issued to him before going absent, and that White had stolen it from him as he knew that Raveney had intended to use it to exact revenge because White had framed him. As they approached Constable Burton White allegedly drew the gun and threatened him; Raveney tried to grab it but as the Land Rover went round a bend, the gun went off. Raveney therefore had a defence of self-defence. When it came to trial, however, the jury at York was confused on what was decidedly thin evidence anyway. Raveney was hanged at Leeds.

Samuel Smith 1930

The day Samuel Smith died he was owed £400, no small beer in those days. He was also in the habit of keeping money around his house in Parkfield Drive off Hull's Anlaby Road. So, there were two perfectly good motives for strangling him, which is exactly what happened one day in November 1930. The evidence was good: his garotte was made of mohair; a wooden lath with a nail through it was found nearby, a man was seen leaving the house at the right time, the killer had wiped his bloody hands on a towel, a hat had been found that had been taken from a wardrobe, and a reward was offered. But all of this led nowhere: Sam Smith's killer was never found.

Thomas Riley 1931

Elizabeth Castle, 53, died in what appears to have been one of the most nonchalant murders ever committed. She lived next door to her step-daughter Minnie Fisher in Kirk Vale, Lepton, near Huddersfield. One evening, December 16th, Minnie and Elizabeth greeted each other as normal and later Minnie heard what she assumed was Thomas Riley coming home to Elizabeth as usual; they had been cohabiting for some four months since 36 year old Riley moved from Wigan, and all appeared well. Then all went quiet at the Castles'; the milk lady, Marian Copley Tolson, knocked next day and got no response; Minnie was unconcerned by the silence, assuming that the couple had gone away for a few days.

Nothing much at all happened until Thomas Riley walked into Leeds Millgarth Police Station, handed over his house keys and told the duty sergeant, Harry James, that he had been 'fed up' and that he had killed Elizabeth Castle with a hammer. Initially, when he was not believed, he lost his temper and shouted: "I'm fed up. I'm telling you the truth. We had a quarrel and I hit her on the head with a hammer." Drink was the cause: a drunken row had erupted when Elizabeth racially abused him calling him an 'Irish bastard'. He snapped and lashed out with the hammer that was nearby.

At 10 o'clock he went to bed and the next day told people that Elizabeth was visiting a sick friend; he then travelled to Leeds where he stayed overnight. On December 18th, Riley moved to Bradford staying at the Salvation Army Hostel, before going to Leeds the following day, to give himself up. His defence of provocation had little impact and he was found guilty of murder and, despite an appeal, hanged.

Twenty-three year old John Henry Roberts, who was convicted of battering to death Alfred Gill at Pudsey was hanged at the same time. It was the last double execution at Leeds.

John Henry Roberts 1931

This atrocious murder became known as the 'piggery killing' after Alfred Gill's battered body was found in one of his piggeries at Tyersal, Pudsey on New Year's Eve 1931. His watch said 6.13, possibly the time of death, and his sons found his body after he failed to return home. Fifty-five year old Gill was a successful grocer with a mobile shop and the piggery. John Roberts was his part-time assistant who was always short of money; on the day that he died, Gill had been walking around with £50 in his pocket. Gill's family was concerned by his unusually long absence. The police were interested.

Earlier that day, Roberts had been seen with one of Gill's horses, and sporting a black eye. At the local, the Ring of Bells, witnesses reported that Roberts had gone home to change his clothes. When the police interviewed him, Roberts confessed that there had been a row in the piggery and that he had smashed Gill on the head with a hammer that was close to hand. Evidence, however, showed that Gill had sustained multiple blows to the head: Roberts hanged at Leeds.

George Emanuel Michael 1931

George Emanuel Michael murdered his wife Theresa Mary Hempstock, 47; he stabbed her to death at her home in Upper Union Street, Hull near Paragon Station on New Year's Eve 1931. George Michael was an Afro-Caribbean from Denmark; he had married Theresa Hempstock in 1929 but she was already married. Later she handed herself in to the police and admitted bigamy. When Michael heard the bad news he said, 'I'll kill her. She's done this to get rid of me'.

When he took a room at 9 Providence Terrace, Walker in Hull he had a conversation in the kitchen with the landlady regarding the rights and wrongs of killing someone. The landlady said 'You mustn't kill anyone. They'll kill you if you do'. They then started to talk about hanging and George Michael said 'In Denmark they don't hang anyone'. The landlady said 'they do here unless it's an accident. You don't want to think things like that, you'll get over it'. Michael said 'I'll never get over it'. He told the landlady how Theresa was married to another man who was still alive and well in Hull, that she was now having an affair and that she had taken all his money. To the landlady Michael seemed obsessive.

On New Year's Eve he went to the post office to take out his money. Later he bought a sheath knife from an ironmongers in Hessle Road. At about 3pm there was a disturbance outside 7 Upper Union Street when Michael demanded that Theresa come out: 'Tell her to come out, I won't do anything to her. By Jesus Christ I'll go to the gallows for her before I leave this fucking street'. A policeman arrived, Theresa Hempstock came to the door and she, George Michael and the policeman went inside. Michael was claiming that Theresa had hid his naturalisation papers which she denied. The licensee of the nearby Drum and Cymbals pub who had been observing all of this went into the pub to get a club. He heard Theresa scream and went into 7 Upper Union Street where he saw Michael with a knife struggling with the policeman; he hit George Michael on the head a few times with the club; as Michael fell down he stabbed himself in the chest with the knife. However, Michael had rained a series of blows on Theresa which ultimately killed her. When the surgeon examined Theresa Hempstock at Hull Royal Infirmary she was dead. The postmortem showed that she had died from a haemorrhage from a large wound to the apex of her left lung. Michael was sentenced to death at Leeds Assizes and hanged at Hull.

The Joseph Swaine Murder 1932

Skipton Auction Market was the unlikely setting for a mysterious murder when 60 year old Joseph Swaine was attacked from behind in the toilets. Amazingly, his battered body remained undiscovered until the next day although in the meantime some well-meaning person found his false teeth and placed them on a stall for safety. Swaine was due to marry 27 year old Gwen Forrest who lived in Queen's Terrace in Otley. The police suspected a gang had committed the murder but they got no further than that until, that is, Thomas Gaunt turned up out of the blue and confessed to the killing. However, it soon became obvious that Gaunt was deranged and his confession was unsafe – but they locked him up in Armley Gaol anyway. The case remains unsolved.

Ernest Brown 1933

Ernest Brown was a groom in the employ of Frederick Ellison Morton of Saxton Grange near Tadcaster. He started an affair with Morton's wife, Dorothy, which ended in murder when Brown cut the phone wires and shot Frederick Morton in the chest in his car in the garage before torching it. There had been a disagreement between the two men, after which Brown resigned, only to beg to be reinstated a few days later. Morton agreed but Brown seemed to resent Morton even more. Brown argued with Dorothy and struck her. A fearful Mrs. Morton and a friend, Ann Houseman, discovered that the phone was dead so they locked themselves in their bedroom. At about 3.30 in the morning they heard a loud explosion when the garage was set on fire. Morton was hanged at Armley Prison in February 1934.

Elizabeth Rhodes 1933

Elizabeth Rhodes's defence was self-defence when she appeared at Leeds Assizes, charged with the murder of her husband with one blow to the head using a heavy long-shafted hammer. The Rhodes's marriage was not a happy one and things came to a head one night in their Hebden Bridge home when Samuel Rhodes turned the radio off when the Irish national anthem was being played. Elizabeth Rhodes was Irish and angered by this; Samuel promised to 'finish her' next time they rowed.

The prosecution argued that she slew him when he was asleep in bed; defence maintained that she struck him as he attacked her. The jury returned a guilty verdict and there was an appeal. It then emerged that Elizabeth was severely affected by her husband's abuse, attempting suicide five times and even jumped in the canal on one occasion in bid to end it all. The appeal judges upheld the original verdict but allowed an appeal for mercy. Elizabeth Rhodes learnt that she was to be reprieved while waiting in Strangeways Prison.

Louis Hamilton 1934

Louis Hamilton was a very violent man; when he and Maud married they moved in with her sister who had to call the police when one day he beat her up very badly. Later he grabbed Maud in Jermyn Street, Bradford and dragged her into the house they were visiting where he cut her throat. Hamilton made no attempt to escape and waited for the police to arrest him; he told them 'I quite realise what I have done'. The case is interesting because his defence tried to argue that Hamilton was having an epileptic fit when he murdered Maud. No one was convinced and Hamilton was hanged at Armley Gaol. Epilepsy was sometimes used by defence counsels to support evidence of insanity.

David Maskill Blake 1934

David Blake lived in Lady Pit Lane, Leeds; at this time he was an out of work steel erector – a bad time to be unemployed because he was soon to be married. Blake considered himself a "…bit of a womaniser"; however, his attentions seemed more forced than welcomed. On 16th October 1934 the night before his wedding to Jean Whitehead, Blake went out walking with a young waitress called Emily Yeomans with the intention of having sex with her. That night, Emily, 23, living with her uncle at Garnet Place, Dewsbury Road, Leeds and working at the Lyons Cafe in the County Arcade, was raped and strangled; her partly-clothed body was found in Middleton Woods. Next day Blake married his fiancée. Bizarrely, he showed his best man, Albert Schofield, a report in the local paper about the Emily Yeomans murder the previous night, an odd thing to do at a wedding. Schofield's suspicions increased the next day when he met Blake at the Mulberry Inn; Blake was with another woman. Schofield was aware that Blake had been out with Emily Yeomans and that the police were looking for a 'man in a blue suit'; Blake was wearing a blue suit on the day of the murder.

Schofield went to the police and Blake was arrested and charged with Emily's murder. The same cat hair and fibres were found on both Blake's suit and Emily's skirt. Moreover, a powder compact identified as Emily's was found at the house where Blake spent the night after the murder.

Blake, 24, was found guilty at Leeds Assizes; the court then learnt that he had previously served a three-year prison sentence after raping, robbing and almost choking to death a woman whom he had offered to walk home after she had missed her bus. Mr. Justice Goddard handed down the death sentence and Blake was hanged on 7th February, 1935 by Thomas Pierrepoint and Alfred Allen. It was later revealed in Parliament that there was a '…violent scene in the condemned cell at Armley Goal, Leeds before the execution of David Maskill Blake' where '…one warder was seriously injured'.

May Brownhill 1935

The first of two mercy killings which took place in Yorkshire in the 1930s. Sixty-two year old May Brownhill lived with Denis, her 30 year old 'imbecile' son in Burn Bridge near Harrogate when she learnt that she needed a life-saving operation, after which she would be unable to provide her son with the care he needed on a daily basis. If she did not have the operation she would be dead in six months and Denis would be on his own in the world.

So on September 17th she made the agonising decision to end Denis' life by giving him 100 aspirins and gassing him in the oven. When arrested, the Inspector in Knaresborough charged her with 'wilfully and maliciously murdering her son'; she replied 'not maliciously, I simply put my boy to sleep'. May had the operation in Salford Royal Hospital and later appeared in court. Her defence council described the 'veritable living death' she had endured. She was convicted of murder at Leeds Assizes; the death sentence was passed with the strongest recommendation for mercy; two days later she was reprieved. At the trial the judge pointed out to May and the court that, while the time may come when an imbecile may be sent legally to a merciful death, that was not the law at the moment and it was not for him or for her to make laws.

The Murder of Oswald Walker 1936

Oswald Walker's skull was smashed when he was attacked from behind and strangled in his George Street tool shop in Hull. Oddly, only one of two purses he had on him was taken and silver and othe valuables had not been stolen. Family life had not been good recently: Walker had recently fired his son, Norman, and his estate was all destined to go to his daughter. However, there was never enough evidence against Norman. A fantasist confused the investigation: he had hitch-hiked in a lorry to the shop from Doncaster but his tearful confession was nothing more than the ramblings of a mentally unstable man. Verdict: murder by person or persons unknown.

John Edwards 1936

John Edwards was an epileptic, and suffered all the symptoms of epilepsy: fitting, periods of deep depression, loss of memory, sporadic violent behaviour. He had difficulty holding down a number of jobs in and around Bradford, the latest being at Newboulds the bakers some seven weeks before he met Myrtle Parker and started taking her out; they frequently went to her parents' house in Bierley. Marriage was discussed and in prospect, although Myrtle's mother advised them to wait as her daughter was still a minor; she was under twenty-one.

One night they went out as usual; oddly, he went off for a while but returned. Myrtle later started to cry and implored him not to leave her; the anxiety this caused him flipped him into an epileptic fit. Deeply depressed, he took out his penknife and whirled it around, not knowing where; he had no recollection of the episode at all. At 5.00 am he turned up at a friend's house, confessing that 'I have done my woman in'.

Despite considerable compelling evidence, medical and otherwise, stacked in Edwards' favour and the absence of any motive – he had killed the woman he loved and was to marry – he was convicted of murder and sentenced to death. Even the expert evidence of one of the country's leading psychiatrists, Dr. Frederick Eurich, a consultant at Bradford Royal Infirmary, cut no ice. Reprieves were not unknown in cases where epilepsy was a factor: in 1870 a man who killed a policeman won a reprieve in Lincolnshire because epilepsy was judged to have caused his actions. But there was to be no reprieve for Edwards. The court heard that four years earlier he had stabbed a woman in the arm during a fit and was given six month's hard labour; epilepsy had also been rejected then as a mitigating factor.

Margaret Peel 1938

Margaret Peel was struck eleven times on the head from behind in her home-cum-village shop in the village of Fewston between Harrogate and Skipton. Her bloodied body was discovered by a young girl neighbour, Ethel Marston. Typically, the prime suspect was her husband Jesse Peel who that morning had left for work at the reservoir as usual and was actually seen there. Jesse could easily have slipped home by a back road but that still left the vexed question of a motive. DC Huddleston was on the case; he made the first ever use of a two-way radio during his investigations.

When Jesse arrived at the scene he actually stepped over his wife's corpse to check if anything had been stolen; in fact £12 was missing. During the immediate detective work he strangely never touched his wife's body once. Then a tyre lever was found at Fewston Reservoir, the murder weapon no less. Jesse was arrested but acquitted through lack of evidence. Jesse Peel died in a car crash soon after and it was only then that any malicious rumours surrounding his guilt abated.

Kathleen Mumford 1938

Another tragic mercy killing. The sad case of Derek Mumford, classified as a 'mental defective' is one of the earliest cases of euthanasia; he was completely disabled and would never be able to help himself in any way. Despite strenuous efforts to have her son properly treated which included carrying him five miles twice a day for a number of weeks from their home in Middleton, south Leeds, Kathleen Mumford was sentenced to death for murder after she gassed Derek in the oven. The press headlined this as 'Murder of Imbecile Son'. She gave Derek sixteen Luminal tablets, the anti-epileptic drug phenobarbital, gassed him and carried him wrapped in a blanket to Leeds Town Hall. He died later in Leeds Infirmary where she tried to prevent attempts to resuscitate him.

Kathleen Mumford had been beside herself and, rightly, could see no dignified or worthwhile future for her son who suffered from Little's disease, a form of cerebral palsy. The best she could get from the authorities was that Derek should be admitted to a 'mental colony' for the rest of his life. Kathleen Mumford knew that this was not the answer and even asked her GP if she could 'do away with the boy'. She knew what she was talking about and wanted to spare him from the abuse and mistreatment she herself had suffered while being raised in a Victorian orphanage in Spennymoor.

Kathleen Mumford was duly convicted of murder; to the judge it was quite simple: murder was murder even though Mumford insisted that she had no regrets regarding her action because she knew that this was the humane thing to do: 'he would never be normal…what was the child to live for? All the days of his life he would have been an imbecile. Was it right that a child should have to live like that? Therefore I ended his sufferings'.

The jury found her guilty of wilful murder but with 'the very strongest recommendation to mercy'. After two years in Aylesbury Prison she was released on pardon and returned to her home town of Darlington. In 2015 a powerful short film based on these events was released: *An Unfortunate Woman*.

Irene Wray 1939

Norman and 33 year old Irene Wray lived in Calverley between Leeds and Bradford; Norman was a philanderer of the first order; Irene loved Norman despite this and pulled out a gun one night to frighten him into some degree of fidelity. She succeeded only in shooting him in the back of the neck, after struggling with the trigger, as later demonstrated in court. Irene reported the incident to her GP; Norman died later in hospital. It emerged later that not only was Norman a serial philanderer but he was often abusive to his wife and to their children. Irene Wray was found not guilty of murder and walked free; the court applauded.

Edna Hague 1939

Edna Hague from Sheffield was also acquitted, but on entirely different grounds. In this case the jury decided that they had heard enough evidence and brought the trial to an end. Edna's father, Alfred, had made a dying oath that he had stumbled and fallen on a knife. What really happened was that Alfred had violently attacked Edna and she stabbed him in self-defence. The judge acquitted her, stating that 'you did what anyone would do if they were in fear of their lives. You are instantly discharged'.

Alfred Burt Clarke 1945

When dressmaker Margaret Ellen Steele, 41, was widowed in 1939 – her husband was killed in the war – she decided to take in lodgers at her house at 4 Grange Terrace in Lightcliffe, Halifax. One such lodger was Captain Burt Clarke. But she had no idea that in 1945, despite being demobbed, 45 year old Captain Clarke, a former RAMC officer, would still be living there – after all, he had a wife and children in Kent to go back to. Margaret wanted rid of him and resorted to a solicitor's letter to speed him on his way. When she went to the house with her solicitor to pick up some clothes before going on holiday, all seemed well: Clarke assured them that he was ready to leave and that his taxi was on the way. However, while both Clarke and Margaret Steele were upstairs the solicitor, a Mr. Taylor, heard a scream. He ran up to find Clarke holding a gun: one shot was fired into Margaret's back, the other into his own chest. Clarke's suicide note and confession was found in the bathroom; it read 'Sorry. You sentenced me to death. Nobby'.

Thomas Eric Richardson 1945

When the body of 41 year-old GP Dr. David Dewar was found under a sack on the driveway of his home in Beeston Road in industrial south Leeds, he was found to have ten axe wounds to his head, seemingly inflicted while he was opening the garage door. Dewar was a popular and respected GP, 'the working man's friend', but there was another side to him, not always consistent with the professionalism usually associated with the medical profession. Dewar liked a night out and those nights were spent in strip clubs and seedy bars like the Silver Slipper Club where the star attraction was Big Bertha. Moreover, Dewar was having an affair of sorts with a woman named Laura; the problem was that Dewar was not alone in this – a local engineer, 27 year-old Thomas Eric Richardson, was also the recipient of Laura's affections.

Richardson confessed to murdering the good doctor and to throwing the axe into the River Aire; he also told Laura what he had done. Despite pleading that he had drunk too much that night and was not responsible for his actions, the jury returned a verdict of guilty with a strong recommendation for mercy. The judge dismissed the plea. Thomas Eric Richardson was hanged on 7th September 1945, by Tom Pierrepoint and Herbert Morris.

Part Two: Murder Matters

The Appeal

An appeal against a judgement has been defined as 'Timely resort by an unsuccessful party in a lawsuit or administrative proceeding to an appropriate superior court empowered to review a final decision on the ground that it was based upon an erroneous application of law'. In murder cases before 1964, when hanging was abolished in the UK, the outcome of appeals was quite literally the difference between life and death. The Court of Appeal was established in 1875; before 1907 a convicted murderer's only hope was a Royal Pardon. In the early years of the 20th century many appeals hinged either on the appellant's sanity or insanity or 'an erroneous application of law'.

Armley Gaol

HM Prison Leeds is a category-B men's prison which opened in 1847 and is still referred to locally as Armley Gaol. The suitably grim looking building, disturbingly visible for miles around, was built with four wings radiating from a central point, each of which had three landings of cells – on the 'then modern penitentiary principal with four radial wings'. It was responsible for incarcerating prisoners sentenced in the West Riding but also took over the gruesome task of executing West Riding prisoners from York Castle. Ninety three men and one woman suffered the death penalty at Armley between 1864 and 1961 – an average of almost one every year. Two new wings were added in 1994, and a new gate complex opened in September 2002. The prison can accommodate up to 1,212 prisoners in 551 normal cells and in six residential units, a segregation unit, First Night Centre, Vulnerable Prisoner unit and in-patients Healthcare Facility.

The last double execution at Armley Gaol was that of Thomas Riley and John Roberts on the 29th April 1932. They were hanged by Tom Pierrepoint; it took 90 seconds to complete. Riley was hanged for the murder of 52 year old Elizabeth Castle with whom he was cohabiting; Roberts was executed for the murder of greengrocer Alfred Gill whom he had battered to death. Double executions stopped in 1954 and were outlawed by the 1957 Homicide Act. The extra time they took subjected the prisoners to unnecessary and avoidable anxiety and suffering.

Arsenic

A poison in a small dose is a medicine, a medicine in a large dose is a poison.
– Alfred Swaine Taylor (1806-1880) toxicologist

If you could have asked a woman in the early part of Victoria's reign who was intent on getting rid of annoying children, her husband, or relatives complicating her inheritance, what her poison was, then she may well have answered 'gin'; but she may also have replied 'arsenic'. Murder by arsenic poisoning perpetrated by women was at epidemic levels in England at the time. It required no real physical effort and it fitted nicely with a woman's role as the preparer of the household's food.

White arsenic or arsenic trioxide (As_2O_3) is a metallic oxide commonly used in the 19th century as a pesticide to kill vermin and insects and as a herbicide, a tonic and as a constituent in medicines, in agriculture as a dip for sheep, and in wallpaper. It was very cheap, freely available up to 1851, odourless, soluble in water and more or less tasteless. William Farr said of it as Statistic Head of the General Register Office in 1840 'that it is generally asked for to kill 'rats', but it is questionable whether arsenic kills more rats than human beings'.

When taken with food the symptoms initially include headaches, confusion, severe diarrhoea, and drowsiness, convulsions and changes in fingernail colour – leukonychia striata (Mees's lines) – this is followed by vomiting blood, abdominal pain, encephalopathy, and watery, bloody diarrhoea – all very similar to the symptoms of cholera and gastro-enteritis. Cholera epidemics were frequent with major outbreaks in 1831-2, 1848-9, 1853-4 and 1866 responsible for the deaths of some 140,000 people; death by arsenic poisoning was, therefore, highly confusable with death by cholera. By the 19th century, arsenic had acquired the nickname "inheritance powder", because impatient heirs used it to confirm or accelerate their inheritances.

In small quantities arsenic is not lethal but its effects are cumulative. In large doses it is fatal although not quick – death usually taking several hours. Masquerading as cholera, and where there were no suspicious circumstances, doctors would often not feel the need for an autopsy. Until 1836 there was no reliable test for detecting arsenic. Then James Marsh, a chemist at the Woolwich Royal Arsenal, published a paper giving detailed methodology for testing for traces of arsenic and for measuring the quantity. Marsh was involved in the case of James Boodle in 1832; Boodle was acquitted in the absence of reliable forensic evidence, although he later admitted poisoning his grandfather's coffee. The Marsh Test soon assumed gold standard forensic procedure status and samples of food, drink, stomach contents and tissue were examined using it. The test was highly sensitive and could detect as little as a 50th of a milligram of arsenic. In 1841 German chemist Hugo Reinsch published a description of a test whereby metallic arsenic was deposited on copper foil from hydrochloric acid solution. The test was easier to perform than Marsh's, as it could be applied to a liquid containing organic matter.

The teaching hospitals embraced these tests, leading to a pool of expert witnesses nationwide becoming available to prosecutors. Once the efficacy of the tests became widely known, they became more of a deterrent and cases of arsenic poisoning eventually began to diminish. However, from 1843 to 1852, 22 women were hanged in England and Wales; no fewer than 17 of these were arsenic poisoners. The nefarious activities of "Sally Arsenic", as Sarah Chesham was dubbed by the media, and of others eventually percolated into Parliament. The Earl of Carlisle introduced the Sale of Arsenic Regulation Bill in early 1851, the terms of which required suppliers to keep a register including the name of the purchaser, the amount bought and the reason for buying it. The purchaser was obliged to sign the register. Vendors could only sell to persons they knew or, if they were not known to them, to persons accompanied by a witness who could verify their identity; they too had to sign the register. Henceforth, arsenic had to be coloured to invalidate the defence that the poisoner had added it to food by mistake. Uncoloured, white, arsenic could only be bought in commercial amounts, that is, a minimum quantity of 10 lbs. The Bill received the approval of the House of Lords the day before Sarah Chesham was hanged; it was originally to have contained a clause outlawing women from buying arsenic, but this was later dropped.

Thomas Askern (1816-1878)

Between 1856 and 1878 Askern was Yorkshire's principal hangman. An ex criminal – as was the custom in recruiting hangmen – Askern was serving time for debt; he numbered amongst his more notorious convicts Mary Ann Cotton, the arsenic serial killer, at Durham in 1873. He did the honours at 20 public hangings and at four private, working at York, Leeds, Lincoln and Durham. His first engagement was the hanging of William Dove at York Castle for the murder of his wife on 9th August 1856. He hanged eight prisoners at York, the last being William Jackson on 18th August 1874.

At Armley Gaol, he carried out the only public executions there when Joseph Myers and James Sargisson were hanged together for separate murders. Askern also officiated at two private executions at Armley. The arrival of the railways allowed Askern to commute easily to Durham where he carried out all five public hangings between 1859 and 1865. The last was the hanging of Matthew Atkinson on 16th March 1865. The rope broke and Atkinson had to be hanged again. Askern was not asked back again by the Sheriff of Durham; he was replaced by William Calcraft.

Askern carried out the last public hanging at Lincoln Castle on 5th August 1859 when he hanged William Pickett and Henry Carey side by side for the murder of William Stevenson. George Bryce, the "Ratho murderer" was the last person to hang in public, by Askern, in Edinburgh, on 21st June 1864, for the murder of Jane Seaton. Askern also officiated at the last public hanging in Scotland when 19 year old Robert Smith hanged on 12th May 1868 at Dumfries, for the murder of a young girl.

Askern carried out Britain's first private hanging of a woman, that of Priscilla Biggadyke at Lincoln in 1868. She was later found to be innocent and was pardoned. In Ireland Askern executed Thomas Montgomery at Omagh on the 26th of August 1873 and John Daly at Belfast on the 26th of April 1876. He hanged James Dalgleish at Carlisle on the 19th of December 1876. His last engagement was at the execution of 37 year old John Henry Johnson at Armley on Wednesday 3rd April 1877 for the murder of Amos Waite. Again the rope broke and Johnson had to be recovered from the pit to be hanged again ten minutes later. In total he carried out 21 public and eight private hangings.

Asylums for the Criminally Insane

The ultimate destination of those murderers who escaped hanging on the grounds of insanity. Until the early 19th century the treatment in these places simply involved restricting the patient and rendering them immobile. But attitudes were changing and in 1813 York Asylum received a damning report which led to a public enquiry. One of the outcomes was that in 1919 Matthew Allen was appointed to take charge at York; the enlightened Allen, who later went on to treat John Clare, advocated 'moral management' of patients which encouraged a tolerant and humane caring environment.

This was all anticipated or echoed by William Tuke, who in 1796 founded The Retreat in York, in which he instigated a revolutionary way of treating the mentally ill: humanely. This was in stark contrast to existing methods which saw patients as being in possession of demons, chaining them up as criminals: they were prisoners rather than patients in a squalid, punitive environment. Tuke wanted 'an institution for the care and proper treatment of those labouring under that most afflictive dispensation, the loss of reason.' His resolve was triggered when the relatives of a Quaker patient, Hannah Mills, were refused visiting rights to the York Lunatic Asylum after Hannah's death there; Hannah had been kept shackled. A delegation of Quakers obtained permission to visit and inspect. Tuke and his Quaker family resolved that never again would a Quaker be forced to endure such treatment.

The 30 bed Retreat was the result: 'a habitation for persons in a state of lunacy', and it laid the foundations for the modern treatment of psychiatric disorders and patients. In 1813 Samuel Tuke described it as 'moral treatment' in his *Description of the Retreat*. The Retreat continues to serve the needs of the psychiatric patient today and remains a highly-respected centre of excellence.

The immoral practice of sending embarrassing and difficult relatives to asylums was also properly regulated from 1890. After the 1959 Mental Health Act the name of Broadmoor was changed from the insensitive Criminal Lunatic Asylum to Special Hospital.

Baby Farming

The absence of effective contraception and the presence of powerful social stigma of having a child out of wedlock are responsible for baby farming, sometimes a sinister, commercial practice which exploded in the late Victorian era to take advantage of vulnerable young women and their babies. Basically, it involved untrained women offering wet nursing, legal fostering and adoption services to unmarried mothers who would hand over their baby with a £10 to £15 cash payment on the promise that the child would be accommodated safely and happily in a new home. Most, no doubt, were: some would be sold to childless couples and others fostered or adopted for a few pounds.

For an unmarried new mother baby farming, or 'putting baby out to nurse' was an attractive option to the enduring shame that an illegitimate brought with it: it was simple, quick and legal with few if any questions asked. Abortion was illegal and back street abortions were notoriously dangerous with countless maternal deaths from haemorrhaging and infection; prosecution and imprisonment awaited the patient if she was discovered.

Interestingly, better-off women were also not averse to putting their infants out to be cared for in the homes of villagers. Jane Austen was fostered like this, as were all her siblings, from a few months old until they were toddlers. Despite the convenience to parents, the practice often inevitably created lifelong emotional distance in the child.

Abandonment was also illegal and attracted little sympathy in the courts to women who abandoned their children in those days. Murdering unwanted children by their mothers usually resulted in a death penalty in Victorian Britain. Selina Wadge was hanged by William Marwood in 1878 at Bodmin for the murder of her illegitimate son, and Louisa Masset was the first person to be executed in the 20th century for murdering her son.

When a "re-homed" baby disappeared, as often happened, the mother was usually too frightened or ashamed to report the matter to the police so unscrupulous baby farmers were easily able to kill off unwanted babies or babies which were hard to foster. Baby murder yielded a quicker profit with no costs incurred for caring for the child. When a baby's body was found, it was often impossible to trace the mother as forensics was in its infancy and there were no DNA tests.

Six baby farmers were hanged in England and one each in Scotland and Wales over the 40 year period from 1870-1909. The tip of a huge iceberg, no doubt. In an attempt to eradicate these practices, the *British Medical Journal* ran a vociferous campaign and Parliament enacted legislation to better protect babies and small children, including the Infant Life Protection Act of 1897, the Children's Act of 1908 and the 1939 Adoption of Children (Regulation) Act. These required that full details of any change of custody or death of a child aged under seven must be notified within 48 hours to local authorities; they empowered local authorities to actively seek out baby farms and lying-in houses, to access homes suspected of abusing children, and to remove children to a place of safety. The new laws also redefined improper care of infants: "no infant could be kept in a home that was so unfit and so overcrowded as to endanger its health, and no infant could be kept by an unfit nurse who threatened, by neglect or abuse, its proper care and maintenance."

Proper regulations relating to adoption and fostering brought an end to baby farming in Britain. The Nazi Lebensborn, "Fountain of Life", programme can be seen as a form of baby farming. Its prevalence can be gauged by its appearances in popular culture. The eponymous hero in Charles Dickens' *Oliver Twist* spends his early years in a baby farm; in the Gilbert and Sullivan opera *HMS Pinafore*, Buttercup reveals that, when she was a baby farmer, she switched two babies of different social classes so satirising class hierarchy in Victorian England. In the Ealing Comedy *Kind Hearts and Coronets* (1949) set around 1900, the hangman Mr. Elliott says "Went up to Manchester on Monday … a poisoner. Baby-farmer at Holloway this morning."

For Whom the Bell Tolls

The bell of the prison, or the bell of the parish or neighbouring church was tolled for 15 minutes after an execution. A black flag was run up on the prison flagpole. This all ended in 1902.

Benefit of Clergy

One sure way to delay the awful day you met your maker on the scaffold was to claim benefit of clergy when charged with capital crimes, including murder. In short, it was the exemption the English clergy and nuns enjoyed from the jurisdiction of the ordinary civil courts, granted by Henry II in the 12th century and abolished in 1823. Under *privilegium clericale* clergymen could be tried instead in an ecclesiastical court under canon law. There the convicted were obliged to undergo a literacy test: the Biblical passage traditionally used was, appropriately, *Psalm 51* (*Psalm 50* according to the Vulgate and Septuagint numbering), *Miserere mei, Deus, secundum misericordiam tuam* – "O God, have mercy upon me, according to thine heartfelt mercifulness". *Psalm 51* became known as the "neck verse" because quoting it could save one's neck. By the end of the 16th century unclergyable offences included murder, rape, poisoning, petty treason, sacrilege, witchcraft, burglary, theft from churches, and pickpocketing.

James Billington (1847-1901)

James Billington was Yorkshire's hangman between 1884 and 1901. Like Henry Pierrepoint he was to found a dynasty of hangmen. James ran a barber's shop in Farnworth near Bolton when not busy with executions. In total he executed 141 men and five women in England and Wales, one man in Ireland and three in Scotland. Billington's debut was at Armley Gaol on the 26th of August 1884, when he hanged Joseph Laycock for the murder of his wife and four children. When Laycock asked him just before he hanged, "You will not hurt me?" Billington replied, "No, thaal nivver feel it, for thaal be out of existence i' two minutes." He carried out seven more hangings at Armley and one at York Castle before succeeding Berry as the executioner for London and the Home Counties in 1892 and then working nationwide.

John Billington (1880-1905)

On the Home Office List from 1902 to 1905. His first execution as "No. 1" was at Strangeways Prison when he hanged Charles Whittaker on the 2nd of December 1903. He hanged John Thomas Kay on the 17th of August 1904 at Armley Gaol, at the same time his brother William was hanging Samuel Holden at Winson Green prison in Birmingham. His last job was at Armley for the execution of Thomas Tattersall on 15th August 1905.

The Bloody Code

Execution by hanging was by no means the exclusive preserve of convicted murderers. The Bloody Code in the late 17th century saw to that when it added a large number of criminal offences to the statute book. In 1688 there were a modest 50 offences on the statute book punishable by death; the number had quadrupled by 1776 and was 220 by the end of the century. Hunting or killing deer were on there and between 1814 and 1834, 68 people were hanged for stealing sheep; a further 1,600 got away with jail or transportation.

Body Snatching, *see* The Resurrection Men or Jerry Crunchers

The Bradford Sweets Poisoning 1858

This was the accidental arsenic poisoning of more than 200 people. Twenty people died and over 200 became seriously ill when sweets inadvertently made with arsenic were sold from a market stall in Bradford. For centuries before, sugar was extremely expensive and was called "white gold". The government recognised the opportunities here and taxed it severely: in 1815 the tax raised from sugar in Britain was £3,000,000. To defray the costs of raw materials , sweet and chocolate manufacturers resorted to adulteration and their products were often mixed with cheaper, substances or 'daft'. 'Daft' was a concoction of harmless substances such as powdered limestone and plaster of Paris.

William Hardaker, known locally as "Humbug Billy", routinely sold his sweets from a stall in the Green Market in Bradford; his supplier, James Appleton, the manufacturer of the sweets – including peppermint humbugs – used 'daft' in his sweet production, 'daft' that was supplied by a druggist in Shipley. Tragically, twelve pounds of arsenic trioxide were sold instead of the harmless 'daft'. Both 'daft' and arsenic trioxide are white powders and look alike; the arsenic trioxide was not properly labelled and negligently stored next to the 'daft'. The mistake went undiscovered during the manufacture of the sweets: Appleton combined 40 pounds of sugar, twelve pounds of arsenic trioxide, four pounds of gum, and peppermint oil, to make 40 pounds of peppermint humbugs. The sweets contained enough arsenic to kill two people per humbug. As usual, Hardaker sold the poisoned sweets from his stall. Of those who bought and ate them, around 20 people died, with a further 200 or so becoming severely ill with arsenic poisoning within a day or so. All involved in the production and sale were charged with manslaughter, but none were convicted. Good did, however, come from this tragedy: there was new legislation to protect the public in the form of the 1860 Adulteration of Food and Drink Bill which changed the way in which ingredients could be used, mixed and combined. The UK Pharmacy Act of 1868 introduced more stringent regulations regarding the handling and selling of named poisons and medicines by pharmacists. The abolition of the sugar tax in 1874 meant sugar became affordable to all, thus making 'daft' redundant.

Capital Punishment

All felonies attracted the death penalty. Capital felonies included murder, manslaughter, arson, highway robbery and larceny. Hanging was the usual punishment although beheading and drowning, usually in a drowning pit, were also deployed, especially for murder.

The Cragg Vale Coiners

The Cragg Vale Coiners (also known as the Yorkshire Coiners) were a gang of counterfeiters in England, from Cragg Vale, near Hebden Bridge. They produced fake gold coins around 1760 to supplement the niggardly incomes they derived from weaving. Coining was literally a licence to make money – simply by clipping coins and making new coins from the clippings. Anyone caught clipping faced the death penalty.

The five man gang was led by "King" David Hartley. This is how they operated: the Coiners got real gold coins from publicans, promising that they could "grow" the investment by smelting the original metals with base ores. Then they clipped off the coins' real edges and milled them again, collecting the shavings and leaving coins that were only slightly smaller than the originals. They then melted down the shavings to produce fakes. Designs were stamped onto the new blank coins with a hammer and a coining kit and the fakes went into circulation. The Cragg Coiners owed much of their success to the fact that their part of Yorkshire was so very remote.

But nothing lasts forever and in 1769, William Dighton, an exciseman, was busy investigating the possibility of a counterfeiting gang operating in Cragg Vale. A coiner called James Broadbent betrayed his colleagues by turning King's evidence and telling the authorities all about the gang. Dighton had 'King' Hartley arrested in the Old Cock Inn in Halifax but Isaac Hartley, 'King' David's brother, plotted to kill Dighton in revenge, offering £100 to anyone who would do the deed. On 10th November 1769, two coiners, Matthew Normanton and Robert Thomas, waylaid Dighton in Swires Road, Halifax and shot him in the head in Bull Close Lane.

Charles Watson-Wentworth (former Prime Minister and Lord Lieutenant of the West Riding) was responsible for bringing the murderers to justice; by the end of 1769 a list of 80 counterfeiters had been compiled, 30 of them from Cragg Vale, 20 from Sowerby, 15 from Halifax, seven from Wadsworth and six from Warley and Midgley. Watson-Wentworth soon had 30 Coiners arrested. David Hartley was hanged at York Tyburn on 28th April 1770, and buried in the village of Heptonstall. His brother, Isaac, was never convicted due to lack of evidence and lived until 1815. Normanton was hanged on 15th April 1775 and Thomas, although acquitted of the murder of Dighton, was finally hanged as a highwayman on August 6th 1774. Their bodies were left chained on Beacon Hill above Halifax for all to see; there was no finer deterrent.

But there was more to this unhappy episode – a savage murder which underlined the lucrative nature of the clipping business and the lengths coiners would go to to preserve that business. When Abraham Ingham informed on a gang of coiners in Heptonstall in 1871 he was trapped by a gang of them in the Cross Inn where an open fire burned brightly. Ingham was led to the fire and red hot tongs were necklaced around his neck before his face and head were thrust into the flames. Red hot coals were then dropped down his trousers and he was spread-eagled over the fire to roast to death.

Definition of Murder

The definition of the *actus reus* (Latin meaning "wrongful act") of murder most usually cited is that by Coke: 'Murder is when a man of sound memory and of the age of discretion, unlawfully killeth within any county of the realm any reasonable creature in *rerum natura* under the King's peace, with malice aforethought, either expressed by the party or implied by law, so as the party wounded, or hurt, etc. die of the wound or hurt, etc. within a year and a day of the same'. The 'year and a day rule' was abolished in 1996. Sir Edward Coke (1552-1634) was an English barrister, judge and politician, the greatest jurist of the Elizabethan and Jacobean years.

Dissection or Anatomisation

The 1751 "Act for the better preventing the horrid Crime of Murder", the "Murder Act", made mandatory the dissection of the bodies of executed murderers or gibbeting for male murderers in particularly serious cases. Seventeen year old Thomas Wilford, who had stabbed to death his wife after one week of marriage, was the first to undergo dissection under the Act after hanging at Tyburn. His sentence read: "Thomas Wilford, you stand convicted of the horrid and unnatural crime of murdering Sarah, your wife. This Court doth adjudge that you be taken back to the place from whence you came, and there to be fed on bread and water till Wednesday next, when you are to be taken to the common place of execution, and there hanged by the neck until you are dead; after which your body is to be publicly dissected and anatomised, agreeable to an Act of Parliament in that case made and provided; and may God Almighty have mercy on your soul."

Fights beneath the gallows were common between dissectionists and the prisoners' relatives over custody of the body. In London, from 1752 to 1809, the bodies were taken to Surgeon's Hall in the Old Bailey where they were publicly anatomised in the lecture theatre, often in front a large audience. The remains of murderer Elizabeth Brownrigg, who hanged at Tyburn in 1767, were kept on display in Surgeon's Hall for many years after her execution. The skeleton of Mary Bateman, "the Yorkshire Witch" hanged at York in 1807, was also preserved in public for years and displayed at the Thackray Medical Museum until 2015. The 1832 Anatomy Act brought an end to this kind of dissection.

John Ellis (1874-1932)

John Ellis was a Rochdale barber and hangman who was on the Home Office list from 1901 to 1923; his relevance to this book is that he did much of his work in Yorkshire. Ellis exemplifies the stress involved in the job and eventually committed suicide. When he came home one night in September 1923 he threatened to kill his wife, took up a razor and slit his own throat.

Ellis particularly disliked hanging women. This came about after he hanged Edith Jessie Thompson at Holloway in 1923 for her complicity in the murder of her husband, Percy, who was stabbed to death by Frederick Bywaters. Thompson was in such a state of hysteria that she had to be carried to the gallows: reports say that "guards had to tie her to a small wooden chair before drawing the noose around her neck", and that "she was hanged in a bosun's chair". Her underwear was soaked in blood after the hanging: the force of the sudden stop as the rope tightened caused a massive vaginal haemorrhage. The large amount of blood, combined with the fact that Thompson had put on weight during her imprisonment even though she had resisted food, suggests she may have been pregnant. There was no postmortem, but thereafter all women when hanged were made to wear canvas pants. Apart from hanging the notorious Dr. Crippen he officiated at the hangings of Thomas Siddle and John Freeman at Hull and Thomas Mead at Leeds. Four hundred people attended Ellis' funeral.

Executions at York

Between 1370 and 1879, 564 convicts were either beheaded or hanged at York. Executions were held on the Knavesmire until 1802 when the Grand Jury, with an eye on the city's tourist image, decided that the 'entrance to the town should no longer be annoyed by dragging criminals through the streets'; the gallows were then transferred to the Castle (The New Drop) and then, in 1868, to a scaffold within the prison nearby. Dick Turpin is, of course, the most notorious Knavesmire, or Tyburn, victim.

In 1746 Duke 'Butcher' Cumberland on his victorious return from bloody Culloden left 70 prisoners here to show his gratitude for the city's hospitality: the Sheriff's chaplain read out the message: 'And the Lord said unto Moses "Take all the heads of the people and hang them up before the sun"'. There was, however, a last minute reprieve – but not for all of the prisoners; lots were drawn to establish which ones would be transported to the colonies instead. Even after that John Jellons was reprieved at the last minute as he was being dragged along Castlegate to the gallows. Twenty-two unlucky Jacobites were nevertheless left to hang for ten minutes, stripped and quartered, their heads stuck on Micklegate Bar, remaining up there until 1754 when they were stolen by Jacobite sympathisers. Twenty or so headless skeletons with disjointed bones were dug up when drains were being built for the Castle jail. Cumberland was awarded the freedom of the city and 100 guineas in a gold box. Cumberland Street in York was named after the butcher Duke.

Forensic Science

The application of science to criminal and civil laws, usually – on the criminal side – during criminal investigation, as governed by the legal standard of admissible evidence and criminal procedure. Since the mid-Victorian era forensic science has become increasingly influential in cases of murder, determining the outcome of a case and sentencing; before 1964 it could make the difference between whether a man or woman in the dock lived or died. Here are some milestones in the development of forensic science:

- The Swedish chemist Carl Wilhelm Scheele perfected a method for detecting arsenic in corpses in 1773 . His work was expanded, in 1806, by German chemist Valentin Ross, who showed how to detect arsenic in the walls of a victim's stomach.

- James Marsh combined a sample made from arsenic, sulphuric acid and arsenic-free zinc, resulting in arsine gas. The gas was ignited, and it decomposed to pure metallic arsenic, which, when placed on a cold surface, would appear as a silvery-black deposit. The test was first described in *The Edinburgh Philosophical Journal* in 1836.

- In 1835 Scotland Yard's Henry Goddard pioneered the comparative use of bullet marks. In a case he was working on, he obsered a flaw in the bullet that killed the victim and was able to trace this back to the mould that was used in the manufacturing process.

- Alphonse Bertillon was the first to apply anthropometry to law enforcement, thus creating an identification system based on physical measurements. Before that criminals could only be identified by name or photograph.

- Bertillon created many other forensics techniques, including forensic document examination, the use of galvanoplastic compounds to preserve footprints, ballistics, and the dynamometer, used to establish the degree of force used in breaking and entering. Although some of his methods were superseded by fingerprinting, other contributions like the mugshot and the systematization of crime-scene photography remain gold standard procedures.

- In 1814 Mathieu Orfila published the highly influential *Treatise on Poisons*.

- In 1858 Sir William Herschel was amongst the first to advocate the use of fingerprinting in the identification of criminal suspects. While working for the Indian Civil Service, he used thumbprints on documents as a security measure to prevent the rampant forging of signatures and went on in 1877 to use fingerprints on contracts and deeds.

- In 1880, Henry Faulds, a Scottish surgeon working in a Tokyo hospital, published his first paper on fingerprinting in *Nature*, highlighting the effectiveness of fingerprints for identification and proposing a method to record them with printing ink. He established their first classification and was also the first to identify fingerprints left on a vial. When he got back to the the UK in 1886, he offered the idea to the Metropolitan Police , but it was dismissed.

- Francis Galton published a detailed statistical model of fingerprint analysis and identification and promoted its use in his *Finger Prints*, 1892; *Decipherment of Blurred Finger Prints*, 1893; and

Fingerprint Directories, 1895. Galton had calculated that the chance of a "false positive" (two different individuals having the same fingerprints) was about 1 in 64 billion.

- The Uhlenhuth test, or the antigen–antibody precipitin test for species, was invented by Paul Uhlenhuth in 1901 and could distinguish human blood from animal blood. The test was further developed for forensic use by the Swiss chemist Maurice Müller in the 1960s.

- DNA fingerprinting was first deployed in 1984, discovered by Sir Alec Jefferys who found that variation in the genetic code could be used to identify individuals and to distinguish individuals from one another.

The Gallows

Hanging at a gallows has always been the method of execution of choice in the UK and Northern Ireland. In 1924 Earl Russell made a case for replacing hanging with gassing on the grounds that gassing would be more humane: official witnesses would not be traumatised and the convicted man or woman would be asleep at the time. It came to nothing, however, when Professor Harvey Littlejohn of Edinburgh University responded by saying that death by hanging was 'absolutely instantaneous' – as we know, this was not always the case.

Early gallows were improvised: trees were used, with prisoners either hauled up manually by the hangman or ladders or horses and carts were deployed which would be removed or driven off, leaving the victim hanging by the neck from a noose. More sophisticated, but not much more, were the two upright beams joined by a crossbar from which nooses were hung, allowing a number of criminals to be despatched at once; relatives would then rush in and pull on the victim's legs to expedite what was otherwise a very slow death.

Gallows were often set up on the western edge of towns or on a local hilltop where the inhabitants would get a good view of the execution. York's Tyburn gallows had been on the Knavesmire from 1379; public executions became a very popular feature of a day at the races. The last hanging there was in 1801 – Edward Hughes was the convict, guilty of rape – after which the gallows were moved to the New Drop near the castle. A paved area with a small plaque today marks where the scaffold was – on Tadcaster Road, opposite Pulleyn Drive. It was originally a gibbet post; the gallows replaced the gibbet in 1379 and remained until finally pulled down in 1812.

Other York gallows were at Gallows Close in Burton Stone Lane under the jurisdiction of the abbot of St. Mary's Abbey and first recorded in 1444-45, demolished by 1802; and at the Horse Fair at White Cross Hill near the present junction of Haxby and Wigginton roads. It was first used in 1690, and was rebuilt in 1693. There were gallows on Foss Bridge administered by the Archbishop of York and those owned by St. Leonard's Hospital on Green Dykes, now Garrow Hill, and close to Thief Lane, along which convicted robbers were led to the scaffold. It is recorded in use from 1374-75 until 1444-45, and redundant by 1500 but in use again from 1571 until 1676, then dismantled in 1700. A gallows belonging to Holy Trinity existed 1150-54 and there was a gallows in the Hull Road, at Gallows Hole, which was abandoned by 1693. At Hull there were tree gallows where the Prospect Street shopping centre now is.

When a crime was committed inside a house, temporary gallows might be erected to hang the criminal at the front door. For cases involving multiple offenders, multiple temporary gallows were erected, with one noose per condemned criminal. In one case we know of a condemned man who suffered an agonising strangulation for 40 minutes until he finally died from asphyxiation.

The famous Tyburn gallows in London – where Marble Arch is now – was triangular, with three uprights and three crossbeams, allowing up to 24 men and women to be executed simultaneously. The Three Legged Mare pub in York is named after a triangular type of industrial gallows which efficiently despatched three felons at once; one was in use at the Knavesmire until 1801 before it was removed in 1812. There is a replica of the 'wonkey donkey' in the beer garden of the pub in Low Petergate. The Last Drop Inn is nearby in King's Square.

In later years, a scaffold with a trap-door was used throughout Britain, through which victims dropped and, in theory, died quickly from a broken neck rather than through strangulation, especially when weights were fixed to their ankles.

Public executions came to an end in 1868 after which hangings were conducted within prison walls in private.

Garotting

The practice of garrotting – which became a popular way to mug someone around 1862 – achieved notoriety in Yorkshire thanks to the murderous activities of Edward Hall in Sheffield. He was arrested for the attempted murder of a coal agent. In addition there was the two man gang in Leeds, operating in Hunslet, who maimed a number of victims and killed two.

The Halifax Gibbet

The gibbet here may well have originated from around 1066. We know that between 1541 and 1650 it was particularly busy with 49 beheadings. It was a stone edifice with stone steps that were thought lost until 1839 when workmen excavated the stone platform.

Gibbeting or hanging in chains was a common law punishment, which a judge could impose in addition to execution; it was regularised in England by the Murder Act 1751, which empowered judges to impose this for murder: "in no case whatsoever shall the body of any murderer be suffered to be buried; the cadaver was either to be publicly dissected or left 'hanging in chains'".

Apart from murderers gibbeting was most often handed down to traitors, highwaymen, pirates, and sheep stealers and was intended as a deterrent to others from committing similar offences. Gibbets were often located next to public highways and crossroads and waterways to maximise visibility. Famously, the body of Oliver Cromwell was gibbeted after his death: monarchists disinterred it at the restoration of the monarchy. Robert Aske, who led the rebellion against Henry VIII known as the Pilgrimage of Grace, was hanged in chains in York outside Clifford's Tower in 1537 for all to see.

One of the last cases of live gibbeting took place near Chatsworth House in the 17th century when a tramp who had killed a woman for not giving him food met his slow and excruciatingly painful death. Tallow and fat would have been larded over his body and a tarred shirt clamped on with iron bands before the obligatory chains were applied. At the time some might have maintained that this was a fitting punishment because the tramp killed the woman by pouring scalding fat down her throat. His screams are said to have disturbed the Duke of Devonshire so much that he called for an end to gibbeting in Derbyshire.

The Hand of Glory

The Hand of Glory was found in Hawthorn Cottage in Castleton's High Street (now a bank). This was the hand of a criminal who died on the gibbet; it was drained of blood, cured in saltpetre and pepper and dried for two weeks; a candle was then placed in its clutch with a wick made from the hair of the corpse and then used by burglars to illuminate the houses they were burgling. The alleged magical properties of the hand ensured that the occupants remained asleep for the duration of the raid; if they did wake they would have been petrified at the sight of the glowing hand. The only way to break the spell was to drench the hand in blood or skimmed milk. Today the hand can be seen in the Pannett Museum at Whitby.

Hanging Ballads

No day out at the gallows was complete without a rousing hanging ballad or two. They were especially popular in Tudor times and a source of income for many a local printer who won the monopoly on their publication. Moral messages and sensational stories based on press reports formed the basis of these macabre singalongs.

The Hangman

The post of hangman was one of the most coveted jobs in the mid 19th century with prodigious numbers, including women, applying whenever a vacancy arose. When William Calcraft retired, the position of hangman for London and Middlesex no longer brought with it a salary. Hangmen were then paid a fee for each execution: £10 for the hangman and 3 guineas for the assistant from the 1880s to the late 1940s, when the hangman's remuneration went up to £15. Rail travel was also reimbursed. Up to 1888 the hangman brought his own rope and pinioning straps and after the execution was also allowed to take the prisoner's clothes and keep the rope. These items could be sold for a considerable amount of money to Madame Tussaud's or to ghoulish members of the public. Half of the fees were paid at the time of the execution; the other half two weeks later. So, no one was in it for the money: most hangmen presumably did it for deeper, more personal, reasons.

After Berry resigned, the Home Office kept a list of available executioners and assistants which was made available to Under Sheriffs when they arranged an execution in their county. For double executions there would normally be two assistants. It was then that all executioners and assistants had to undergo a week's training, first at Newgate and then at Pentonville Prison. If deemed suitable successful novices would attend an execution or two as second assistant, just to observe and for the governor to observe them and their reaction to the hanging. Successful candidates had to sign the Official Secrets Act and were not allowed to divulge any details of what occurred in the execution chamber, especially to the press.

The Hangmen of Yorkshire

York had its own hangman in the 18th century, appointed from the inmate population. Between 1802 and 1835, John (or William) Curry, or Curry Wilkinson officiated there. He was known as "Mutton Curry" and had twice been convicted of sheep stealing, having had his death sentence at the Knavesmire commuted on each occasion. On the second occasion, he was awaiting transportation when the post of hangman became vacant and he accepted it, carrying out the hanging of three men on the 8th of August 1802 for stealing sheep, cattle and from a dwelling house, respectively. By 1810 he had performed 25 executions, including a number of convicted Luddites from Cartwright's Mill at Rawfolds, as described in Charlotte Bronte's 1849 *Shirley*. All did not always go well though. In all, Curry was responsible for at least 63 verifiable executions during his 33 year reign, which ended with a triple execution on Monday, 6th April 1835, when Ursula Lofthouse, Joseph Healy and William Allott were hanged for murder. Lofthouse had murdered her husband.

As a convicted felon, Curry remained a prisoner himself until 1814. He found his job stressful and took to drinking a lot of gin to steel himself for the task. On April 14th 1821, he was called upon to perform two executions. First he hanged highwayman Michael Shaw at York Castle and then had to walk across town to execute William Brown for burglary at the City Gaol. He was somewhat drunk by the time he got there and while waiting on the platform for the prisoner to appear, he began shaking the noose at spectators calling out to them: "Some of you come up and I'll try it!" When Brown appeared, Curry had to be assisted by a warder and one of the Sheriff's officers. "The executioner, in a bungling manner and with great difficulty (being in a state of intoxication), placed the cap over the culprit's face and attempted several times to place the rope round his neck, but was unable. He missed the unfortunate man's head with the noose every time that he tried. The cap was each time removed from the malefactor's face, who stared wildly around upon the spectators"

The *Times* reported on April 24th. The crowd were not amused by this and called out, "Hang him, hang Jack Ketch" (the generic name for the hangman).

On September 1st 1821 Curry was booked to hang five men at one time. The execution was reported by *The Yorkshire Gazette* as follows: "On Saturday last, a few minutes before 12 o'clock, the unfortunate men were conducted from their cells to the fatal drop. After a short time spent in prayer they were launched into eternity. None of them seemed to suffer much. However, by an unaccountable neglect of the executioner (Curry) in not keeping sufficiently clear of the drop when the bolt was pulled out, he fell (into the trap) along with the malefactors." He retired, 20 hangings later, *otium sine dignitate* to the Thirsk Poor House in 1835. *The Yorkshire Gazette* pointed out that 'gin was apt to provide a snare for him'.

Curry was succeeded by James Coates, who was also a prisoner at York, having been sentenced to seven years' transportation for larceny at the summer assizes of 1835. He executed Charles Batty in 1836 and Thomas Williams the following year, both for attempted murder. He managed to escape from the Castle around 1839 and was never heard of again. Due to the unavailability of William Calcraft, who was booked for an execution at Stafford on the same day, prisoner Nathaniel Howard took over the post in 1840 and hanged James Bradsley for the murder of his father on the 11th of April of that year. He went on to hang a further 17 men between then and 1853 when he bungled the hanging of murderer Henry Dobson so badly that, "when the drop fell and the rope tightened around his neck, the condemned man struggled violently" for which apparently Howard was dismissed. He was by this time old and ill and died six days later. There were no executions at York between April 1853 and 1856 and a new executioner had to be found to hang 28 year old William Dove for the murder of his wife on 9th August 1856, as Calcraft was again busy elsewhere. Thomas Askern, who was in prison for debt at the time, was appointed to the role and continued in office until 1868 performing eight executions at York including the last one in public, that of Frederick Parker on 4th April 1868.

Executions at York had decreased markedly with the opening of Armley Gaol in Leeds, which became the place of many Yorkshire hangings from 1864 to 1961. Askern died in Maltby at the age of 62 on December 6th, 1878, ending the practice of York using their own hangman. William Marwood officiated at the next five executions up to 1882. James Berry was used for the execution of James Murphy on the

29th of November 1886. James Billington carried out the final three hangings here, the last being that of August Carlson on the 22nd of December 1896.

A number of hangmen came from Yorkshire but never, or rarely, ever, worked in their home county; they include Bartholomew Binns from Dewsbury (1839-1911); James Berry of Heckmondwike (1852-1913); Thomas Henry Scott, Huddersfield, a rope maker and a stone mason by trade; Henry Albert Pierrepoint (1878-1922) from Bradford; Albert Pierrepoint from Clayton near Bradford (1905-1992).

Highway Robbery

Swift Nick Nevison and Dick Turpin were, of course, not the only highwaymen who preyed on travellers in Yorkshire – and who ultimately paid the price for their troubles. Stockton on the Forest north east of York in the Forest of Galtres had the privilege of seeing Barnhard Siegfred's rotting body gibbeted in the village after being hanged for highway robbery and the attempted murder of John Dolland in 1570.

This obviously escaped the notice of four more highway robbers in 1574 when they waylaid Baron de Cavallo on his way back to York from Penrith via the same dangerous forest. Robert de Fleury and George and William de Abbot were hanged on the Knavesmire but escaped the gibbet, their bodies being sent for dissection instead. A similar fate awaited Mark Trumble from Ripon and Robert Martinson from Haxby when they were convicted of highway robbery at Shipton on the York to Thirsk road; they hanged at the Knavesmire and were buried in St. Olave's graveyard in York's Marygate. As it did Amos Lawson who ill-advisedly held up the Sheriff of York, William Taylor in the Forest of Galtres. His execution at the Knavesmire attracted great crowds 'more a fair for business and pleasure than a place of execution'. Lawson was buried in St. George's off Walmgate. George Melrose was going through the forest in 1661 when he was accosted by Jeremiah Balderson and Richard Souly – worse still, they cut off his nose as well. The criminals were buried in Holy Trinity, Goodramgate.

Conyers Lane on the A684 between Constable Burton and Patrick Brompton near Leyburn is where Leonard Wilkinson ambushed Nicholas Carter of Crakehall and relieved him of the money he had taken at Leyburn cattle market in 1826. Wilkinson also relieved Carter of his life and hanged at the New Drop at York Castle. The deed is commemorated by the Nichol's Stone, or Murder Stone, which lies near the murder site and starkly tells us 'May 19, 1826 Do No Murder'.

The West Riding House of Correction, Wakefield

One of the characteristics of a house of correction was the treadmill and the 'screw', the warden who tightened it. Wakefield was no exception. Prisoners were forced to turn the wheel so many times a day, the tension of which was manipulated by the 'screw'. The prison at Wakefield was established in 1595 as the West Riding House of Correction. Its main purpose, like other county prisons, was detention rather than punishment with most prisoners held on remand until trial and sentence of transportation or death was delivered. When transportation to the American colonies ended with American independence, prisons began to be used for the punishment of offenders, as well as for remand – a policy which increased the prison population. Wakefield took in prisoners from all over the West Riding until 1847, when Leeds Borough opened Armley.

The Wakefield prison has earned the nickname the "Monster Mansion" because of the large number of high-profile, high-risk sex offenders and murderers resident there. The exercise yard there has a mulberry tree, around which female inmates routinely exercised and is the origin of the nursery rhyme "Here We Go Round the Mulberry Bush". In 1873 there were 1,825 women inmates in Wakefield; there were only ever ten executions, the last in 1915, all men.

Houses of Correction in York

There were a number in York: in 1569 weaving-shops were installed at both St. George's House and St. Anthony's poor houses. In 1576 St. George's was converted into a house of correction and in 1577 both it and St. Anthony's 'were provided with mills for the forcible employment of the roguish'.

There were houses of correction on Old Baile from 1807, and another on Toft Green from 1814. The provision of a tread-wheel here seems to have exercised the authorities for some time before one was installed in 1825 – 'a terror to evil-doers'. A typical wheel would have been five feet in diameter with 24 steps holding 24 convicts taking 45 steps per minute for ten hours in the summer and seven in winter. The (often disregarded) maximum was limited to 12,000 feet in ascent in one day or just under three miles. Many simply 'ground air' but at Toft Green the authorities found a commercial angle when they used it in an adjacent bone house for (animal) bone crushing. Unfortunately, the wheel here was also often used as a ladder of escape necessitating its removal from the wall; it was taken away completely in 1833 and prisoners reverted to smashing boulders.

Hulks

A hulk moored eerily in the Thames or in a Suffolk estuary was often the first stop for Yorkshire prisoners destined for Australia or Van Diemen's Land, with hulks located at Sheerness, Woolwich, Chatham, Deptford and Portsmouth. The aptly-named *Retribution* at Sheerness accommodated 600 prisoners. Strict discipline and high levels of hygiene were, apparently, enforced on these vessels of doom. On the hospital hulks, doctors sold corpses for £5. For a few convicted murderers, transportation to Australia or Van Diemen's Land, Tasmania, was a seemingly attractive alternative to hanging. It was, nevertheless, often a one-way ticket to hell with atrocious conditions on board the ships destined for the southern hemisphere. The first fleet left in 1786; transportations continued until 1868.

Hull Prison

Hull opened in 1870 to house men and women. In the Second World War it was a civil defence depot and military prison. In 1955 it was a borstal. The only woman to be hanged at Hull was Ethel Major of Kirby on Bain in Lincolnshire. She was convicted of poisoning her abusive and often drunk husband, 44 year old lorry driver Arthur, with strichnyne. When Arthur demanded to know who the father was of Ethel's daughter, Auriel, who was passed off as Ethel's sister and brought up by her parents, things went from bad to worse.

The executed of Hull:

Arthur Richardson, 30, on March 25th 1902. Murdered his aunt.

William James Bolton, 44, on December 23rd 1902. Stabbed his former girlfriend to death.

Charles William Aston, 19, on December 22nd 1903. Shot his former partner.

Thomas Siddle, 29, on August 4th 1908. Cut his 22-year-old wife's throat.

John Freeman, 46, on December 4th 1909. Murdered his sister.

William George Smith, 26, on December 9th 1904. Killed a woman he was "on friendly terms with" in front of her three children.

Hubert Ernest Dalton, 39, on June 10th 1925. Murdered a colleague.

George Emanuel Michael, 49, on April 14th 1932. Stabbed his partner several times in the head and throat, before attempting to kill himself.

Roy Gregory, 28, on January 3rd 1933. Murdered his two-year-old step- daughter. He struck her over the head with a hammer, before hiding her body in the cellar behind a wall. Her body lay undiscovered for five months.

Ethel Lillie Major, 43, on December 19th 1934. Killed her husband by poisoning his corned beef with strychnine.

Infanticide

Infanticide is defined legally as the crime of a mother killing her child within a year of birth. By the mid 19th century, people were starting to ask how could a mother, defined by her maternalism, murder her children unless she were mad? Infanticide, therefore, was part of an insanity defence. Hogarth's famous *Gin Lane* says it all in one scene: an infant falls from her mother's arms as a result of drink and poverty combined with drudgery, fatigue and serial childbearing – sometimes capped with an abusive husband and mental issues. Until 1803 infanticide cases were tried under a 1624 statute which assumed the offence was committed by an unmarried woman. Furthermore, on the male side, rape-murders of children were not that uncommon – after all, from 1275 it was legally permitted for men to have sex with children so long as they were over the age of twelve; in 1875 this limit was increased to age thirteen and then to sixteen in 1885.

The Foundling Hospital in London opened in 1756 to take in a small number of the illegitimate children. However, the conditions there were lamentable and Parliament withdrew funding and compelled the governors to be self-sufficient, resulting in a draconian admissions policy, with the committee requiring that the hospital: 'Will not receive a child that is more than a year old, nor the child of a domestic servant, nor any child whose father can be compelled to maintain it'. Moreover, once a mother had admitted her child to the hospital, the hospital did everything in its power to ensure that the parent and child were never re-united.

The living conditions of the Industrial Revolution in the north of England served only to exacerbate and give focus to an old problem: children had always been murdered, or deserted for the parish to deal with. Now the new, emerging cities bred a virtual epidemic of child murders, peaking in 1850 and 1860 when, as Henry Humble tells us, people were afraid to examine bundles and sacks left in the street for fear of what they may contain.

Education, or a lack of it, had a role to play. A doctor from Wath near Rotherham, Edmund Syson, appearing before the 1871 Parliamentary Select Committee set up to examine the problem, revealed that he had been approached by an otherwise humane and highly proficient and professional midwife to kill a baby as it was being born. Syson doubted if it had even occurred to the woman that what she was advocating was a crime. These were ordinary women performing a service and, although they were sometimes branded as 'ogresses', 'hags' and 'beldams', they just got on with it. Illegitimates, he confirmed, were disposed of in a procedure euphemistically termed 'going home' – considered to be well worth the trouble it saved the mother in the longer term.

Methods of effecting infanticide were many and sickeningly various. Suffocation – usually effected by lying on or over – but sometimes through airways plugged up with paper, mud, cloth or dough, pushing the baby's face into a pillow or covering the face with a wet cloth; trauma, especially to the head and neck as this could be ascribed to a difficult delivery; fractured skulls caused by dropping the baby 'accidently'; strangulation with various ligatures including the umbilical cord (for which there were many legitimate precedents); puncturing vital organs with fine needles – the preserve of the midwife as a knowledge of anatomy was required, but hard to detect; drowning- with a newborn delivered directly into a bucket of water, confusable with a still birth, all played their part; as did so-called surprise deliveries where baby is delivered into the fetid privy when the mother 'confuses' labour pains with bowel movements. In 1870 a Dr. Wynter observed that he was not the first to note that through 'accidental' drowning, the number of babies which 'left this world on washing days was 'remarkable'.

Burning was a popular way of disposing of the bodies when the worst a midwife could be charged with was unlawful disposal under the Cremation Act after 1884. In 1906 the proprietress of a maternity home boasted she had burned 'dozens' of babies; in the same year a Tottenham baby farmer, while being prosecuted for not registering births, was found to have burned babies' bodies in her kitchen stove. Midwives were sometimes implicated in baby-farming where they would have the baby adopted on payment of a fee from which she would take a hefty commission before passing baby and reduced fee on to the new parents – this was known as 'baby sweating' and the deals were called 'railway station adoptions', for obvious reasons: it was difficult to trace anything back if this nauseating traffic in human life was conducted on an anonymous railway platform.

Cases of infanticide in Britain in the 18th and 19th century can often attributed to the economic position of the women, with sympathetic juries committing pious perjury in numerous murder cases. But the plain reality was, if the woman chose to keep her illegitimate child, society was not set up to mitigate the pressures on the woman, legally, socially or economically. The stigma of illegitimacy – bastard children – played its part, with Georgian and Victorian mothers drowning, and killing by other means, their babies. At the end of the 19th century, physicians and lawyers were beginning to understand more the consequences of puerperal insanity with convictions of murder being commuted to manslaughter and a growing reluctance to hang women.

There were strenuous efforts to identify the fathers of bastard children to ease the burden on local communities and on the mothers. Assistance was available through maintenance payments from the father, but this was capped at a niggardly 2/6d a week. When the father got into arrears with the payments he was only obliged to pay a maximum of thirteen weeks arrears. Whatever happened, women were subjected to the usual complaints that they were benefitting from a free handout; but evidence from Yorkshire shows this not necessarily to be the case: in Leeds in 1822 relief was limited to 1s per week; Sheffield required women to enter the dreaded, squalid workhouse already overcrowded with young mothers and their infants, whereas Halifax gave no relief at all. Fathers often fled the scene, as it were, putting more pressure on the deserted mother and introducing the additional, tragic, option of infanticide. At the same time, when an alleged father was being pursued for payment of maintenance but was sinking deeper into arrears, then the disposal of the child was one way to end the problem, as in the case of Alfred Waddington in 1852.

Servant girls were particularly vulnerable; who knows how many were reduced to this position by rape or blackmail? A servant girl, if she wanted to move on or better herself, relied entirely on good references from her employer. She had no recourse to the relative anonymity enjoyed by factory girls. Hence the sight of many a servant girl standing in the dock on charges of infanticide.

Baby farmers too owe their sorry existence to the absence of community care: in 1906 Annie Scruton from Wakefield gave birth to a baby she could not support so she paid Mary Robson from Bridlington to adopt the child. Robson collected the baby, but while waiting for a train at Normanton, baby fell ill and died on a bench in the waiting room. At the inquest the verdict was neglect, rather than manslaughter.

It was not just women either: the case of John Gowland, a disputatious, aggressive, man in 1860 Bradford is typical of infanticide committed by a man. A bigamist, he was accused of murdering his two children and attempting to kill his wife. The pressure of raising his children just got too much and he attacked them in a fit of insanity.

The Infanticide Act of 1922 made the killing of an infant child by its mother during the first months of life a lesser crime than murder, and no longer a capital crime due to psychological considerations. The Acts of 1938 and 1939 abolished the earlier act, but introduced the idea that postpartum depression was legally to be seen as a form of diminished responsibility: "at the time of the act or omission the balance of her mind was disturbed by reason of her not having fully recovered from the effect of giving birth to the child or by reason of the effect of lactation consequent upon the birth of the child."

As a footnote, it is worth pointing out that today 10,000 women a year in the UK are diagnosed with post natal traumatic stress disorder – 2% of all births. How many women in previous generations were hanged as a result of actions triggered by similar disorders?

Instruments of Torture

In June 1899 an advertisement appeared in the *Yorkshire Herald* for what promised to be a riveting night out: 'A series of lectures upon object lessons, consisting of actual instruments of torture now sanctioned by the Roman Church used by the Romanizing clergy'. Exhibits included a 'Spiked Iron Cage from the Kilburn Sisterhood, used for the Incarceration of Children in their Orphanages; hair Shirts, Rope, Steel Whips, Armlets, steel with sharp points, Cinctures'. Admission was free; questions were invited; lectures were given by…members of the Protestant Alliance.

Kidcotes and York's Other Prisons

The first reference to a civic prison in York is in 1248. Kidcotes is a colloquial name for a prison, two of which were on York's old Ouse Bridge, the first of which was mentioned in 1279. The Sheriff ran one for felons; the mayor the other for drunks and harlots, men and women, clerical and lay, until they could be brought before a court . The city butchers guarded them by night and the bailiffs took over during the day. We know of the following who were incarcerated by the sheriff: the man charged with stealing the keys of Bootham Bar in 1489, a suspected murderer in 1522, and persons accused in 1536 and 1569 of 'reviling the mayor'. A man found posting slanderous bills in 1536 was committed to the mayor's.

Margaret Clitherow was held on old Ouse Bridge before her trial. There was also a kidcote at Wakefield. In the 16th century the city maintained other prisons besides the kidcotes, including one near the city moat, in the the Bean Hills area, mid-way between Fishergate and Walmgate Bars. It accommodated men and women, and took in recusants and in 1606 vagrants. It may have been in the guardroom of Fishergate Bar which later was called Bean Hills Gate. In 1577 Monk Bar was made into a prison and in 1585 a prison on the King's Staith was opened for trespassers on the staith.

York was unique in that it also had Davey Hall in Daveygate, the function of which was to stock the king's larder in York with game and domestic animals. Davey Hall also had a prison for the incarceration of anyone convicted of offences in the King's Forest, the Forest of Galtres, and the only special forest prison known to history. An example of offenders would be venison trespassers in 1289 in 1370 and 1389.

In 1285 the Minster Close was enclosed by a twelve feet high wall within which the Dean and Chapter held sway and, until 1839, had a Liberty of their own – the Liberty of Saint Peter and Peter Prison which, in turn, had its own Chief Constable, constables, coroners, magistrates, bailiffs, stewards and under-stewards. After the Jonathan Martin fire of 1829 the Dean and Chapter decreed that 'Henceforward a watchman/constable shall be employed to keep watch every night in and about the cathedral'.

Minster Police predate the establishment of Sir Robert Peel's police force; indeed, Peel will have been influenced by the Minster Police when he visited his sister who was married to the then Dean, William Cockburn. York Minster is one of seven cathedrals in the world which have their own constabulary or police force. The others are Liverpool's Anglican Cathedral; Canterbury, Hereford and Chester Cathedrals; St. Peter's Basilica in Rome (the Swiss Guard) and Washington's National Cathedral. Today there are ten Minster Policemen at York; they do not carry batons or handcuffs: their non-combative role is to look after over 380 sets of keys, to provide tourist information; security for cash and fire protection. The phrase 'taking a liberty' stems from the police here when in the 13th century the Lord Mayor persisted in entering the Liberty of St. Peter to harass the residents. The Pope intervened to stop him 'taking a liberty'.

Peter Prison (or Seyntepetreprisons as it was sometimes called) was reached through Peter Gate, one of four gates leading in to Minster Close or the Liberty of St Peter, a walled area around the Minster; it was demolished in 1827. Jonathan Martin was one of the last detainees, by which time a report found it in 'a wretched state'. The other three gates were in Ogleforth, the entrance to St. William's College and at Minster Gates.

The archbishop could boast a prison in York by 1351 – the 'bishop prison' or 'convict prison' for criminal clerks and those who had successfully pleaded clergy; it was in the archbishop's palace in 1385 probably in the crypt below St. Sepulchre's Chapel. When the chapel, which had been converted into a public house, The Hole in the Wall, was demolished in 1816, a prison was discovered beneath it.

St. Mary's Prison stood in the Liberty of St. Mary from 1289. It included a debtors' prison at the north gate of the abbey and a courtroom.

Knavesmire: the York Tyburn

York's first gallows were at the Liberty of St. Mary's Abbey. In 1379, however, the citizens of York fell out with the monks and built their own gallows. This was placed 'where the gibbet post stood' on the west side of Knavesmire opposite York Moor (Hob Moor), and assumed the name of the York 'Tyburn'. Between 1370 and 1879, 564 criminals were executed at York. The Knavesmire gallows were used in the hanging, drawing and quartering of scores of York Catholic martyrs; after London's Tyburn, York was the second most prolific place for martyrdom in the land.

Executions were held on the Knavesmire until 1800 when the Grand Jury decided that "Thus will be removed from one of the principal roads leading to the city that disagreeable nuisance, the gallows; and thus will the inhabitants and passengers be no longer interrupted, and their humanity hurt, by the dragging of unfortunate people to the place of execution". The gallows were then transferred to the

Castle (The New Drop) between the castle walls and St. George's field and then, in 1868, to a scaffold within the prison nearby.

The sales opportunities at a public hanging back then were much the same as you would expect to see today at a music festival or football match. The huge crowds could buy pies and beer, chapbooks, last speeches ballads. Other forms of entertainment were put on to keep the crowds happy; bookmakers took bets on the lifespan of the victim once the trapdoor was open.

Private Edward Hewison of Stockton has the dubious privilege of being the first man to be executed at the Knavesmire; he was serving in the Duke of Northumberland's Light Horse when he raped 22 year old Louise Bentley at Sheriff Hutton; she was a servant at the castle making her way to York. Hewison was arrested and executed in what turned into a celebrity hanging next day on March 31st 1379 and gibbeted near Sheriff Hutton. With amazing coincidence, the last man to be hanged there 400 years later was a Private Edward Hughes of the 18th Light Dragoons executed on 29th August 1801 – for also raping a girl.

If you were a noble, you would have been beheaded at the Knavesmire, rather than hanged. Hanging, drawing and quartering was available for those who committed high treason.

Laudanum

Also known as opium tincture, laudanum is a powerful, bitter tasting oral formulation of morphine. Accidental or deliberate overdose was and is common; overdose and death may occur with a single oral dose of between 100 and 150 mg of morphine in a healthy adult – the equivalent of between two to three teaspoons of laudanum. Overdose can result in severe respiratory depression, collapse and death. Victorian women were prescribed the drug, marketed as 'women's friends', for problems with menstruation and childbirth, and even for fashionable female maladies of the day such as 'the vapours', which included hysteria, depression and fainting fits. Nurses spoon-fed laudanum to infants as a soporific. Twenty or 25 drops of laudanum could be bought for a penny.

William Marwood (1820-1883)

Marwood held the office of hangman from 1872-1883. He is important to the 'art' of hanging everywhere because he introduced the "long drop" method of hanging to England, as developed by surgeons in Ireland. If the prisoner were to be allowed a drop of 6 to 10 feet depending upon his weight and with the noose in the right place, death would be "nearly instantaneous" because the neck would be broken. The long drop banished the gruesome and undignified struggling and was far less cruel to the prisoner and less of an ordeal for the governor and staff who, after the abolition of public hangings, had to witness the spectacle at close quarters.

Marwood officiated at five York hangings between 1878 and 1882. He also carried out the last public hanging in the British Isles when he executed Joseph Le Brun at St. Hellier on Jersey on the 11th of August 1875. The 1868 Act requiring executions to be carried out in private in Britain had not included the Channel Islands. During his eleven years, Marwood hanged 179 people, including eight women and fourteen double executions, three triples and one quadruple (at Newgate). He worked without an assistant most of the time. One of his most notorious cases was Charles Peace, burglar and murderer, whom Marwood hanged on 25th February 1879 at Armley Goal.

Mercy

The Royal Prerogative of Mercy – reprieving people who had been sentenced to death – was exclusively in the gift of the reigning monarch up to 1837. Outside London, including Yorkshire, the judges submitted their report and recommendations to the Secretary of State after each Assize. In March 1782 the Home Office was created and the Home Secretary became part of the King's "Hanging Cabinet" which decided the fate of each person sentenced to death. After 1837 the Home Secretary exercised the Royal Prerogative on behalf of the monarch. In 1823 Parliament passed the Judgement of Death which gave judges the power to reprieve in capital felony cases, but not murder. The death sentence was formally recorded and then commuted in open court.

Up to 1838 many crimes carried a mandatory death sentence which could have led to the wholesale judicial slaughter of minor criminals, and revolution. The English kept a cautious eye on France where excessive and cruel punishments were a contributory cause of the French Revolution.

Astonishingly, 11,305 death sentences were handed down in the decade 1826-1835 alone, but only 154 of these were for murder. Fortunately, only 514 (4.54%) were carried out. The next decade saw a sharp decline in both death sentences and executions. Post 1835 the execution rate stabilized at 11.2 per annum for the rest of the century, because the number of capital crimes had been dramatically reduced between 1812 and 1834. In reality, only murderers were sentenced to death after 1861: hanging remained the mandatory sentence for those convicted of murder although many of those sentenced to hang were reprieved where the murder was considered to be less heinous or where there were mitigating circumstances.

Between 1900 and 1958 everyone convicted of murder was still automatically sentenced to death. 1,485 people were sentenced to be hanged for murder and 755 were actually executed. The rest, almost half, were reprieved (49.2%). This was made up of 1,340 men, 741 of whom were subsequently hanged (55.3%). As for women, 145 were sentenced to death but only fourteen hanged, a reprieve rate just over 90%. Ten years in prison was the average stretch for those who were reprieved between 1900 and 1966; nothing short of a bargain, compared with death. Where a trial judge recommended mercy, the Home Office usually listened. The Royal Commission on Capital Punishment (1949-1953) shows that between 1900 and 1949 the judge's recommendation to mercy was overruled only six times. Juries, of course could add a recommendation to mercy to their guilty verdict; between 1900-1949, 1,210 death sentences were handed down with the jury recommending mercy in 460 of them. 112 of the 460 were hanged.

Between 1829 and 1899, 231 women were sentenced to hang in the British Isles which included Ireland. 101 were actually executed, 97 for murder, one for attempted murder, one for conspiracy to murder (in Ireland) and two for arson. Three women were found insane and sent to Bedlam or Broadmoor. One was given a free pardon and one took her own life in the condemned cell. The reprieve rate was 56.3%. From 1861 to 1899, there were to be 119 women given the death sentence of whom 28 were to be hanged for murder, making a reprieve rate of 73.5%.

Micklegate Bar, York

The place for centuries in York to stick severed heads of rebels and traitors. Heads and quarters of traitors were routinely displayed on the top. Most famously: Lord Scrope of Mastan in 1415 after failing to assassinate Henry V; Sir Henry Percy (Hotspur) after his part in the rebellion against Elizabeth I in 1403; Richard, Duke of York after the Battle of Wakefield in 1460, prompting Shakespeare to write: "Off with his head and set it on York's gates; so York did overlook the town of York" (Queen Margaret in *Henry VI*); Thomas Percy in 1569 – his head remained there for two years.

Removal of heads without permission was, appropriately, punishable by beheading – guess where the heads ended up. The last displays were in 1746 after the Jacobite Rebellion at Culloden. The heads of James Mayne and William Connelly remained on the Bar until 1754.

Richard of York was further humiliated while on the Bar with a paper crown. After the battle of Towton on 29th March 1461 the victorious King Edward IV regained the crown for the House of York. He then removed the head of his father Richard and replaced it with some of the captured leaders of the House of Lancaster. Heads were parboiled and seasoned with cumin to preserve them and extend their use as a deterrent and, unsuccessfully, to deter carrion.

Murderesses in the Early 20th Century

Files on seventeen murderesses were published by the National Archives at Kew in 2004, including prison records and pictures never previously in the public domain. They shed new light into what compelled these women to kill their partners or children and babies. The Open Government Initiative relaxed the laws on releasing Home Office files so they are no longer withheld for 100 years in serious criminal cases. These cases were originally subject to closure for 100 years due to the medical and domestic details they contained; they could not be released during the lifetime of the prisoners and, in some cases, their immediate family.

Only in one case, that of Dorothea Waddingham, a nurse from Nottingham, was the convicted hanged, in 1936 for murdering an elderly widow and her disabled daughter. She was one of only twelve women in England to be hanged in the 20th century. The other sixteen had their death sentences commuted to life imprisonment on the direction of the Home Secretary.

An Irishwoman, Elizabeth Rhodes, was driven insane by her violent husband and by period pains. She shattered his skull with a single massive blow from a hammer at their Hebden Bridge farmhouse in 1933. After being reprieved and spending only three years in jail, she was released on parole.

Particularly upsetting was the case was of Edith Proctor, who starved her partner's child to death over a prolonged period. She forced seven-year-old Nellie to spend most of her time in a small back bedroom and deliberately gave her little to eat. The youngster died weighing just 18lbs. Proctor's death sentence was commuted to life imprisonment because she was pregnant at the time, she pleaded her belly.

Oxalic Acid

Oxalic acid is harmful and potentially lethal if swallowed; it destroys tissue and burns if absorbed through the skin or is in contact with the eyes. Symptoms include a burning sensation, cough, wheezing, laryngitis, shortness of breath, spasm, inflammation and oedema of the larynx, inflammation and edema of the bronchi, pneumonitis, pulmonary oedema. The lethal oral dose is 15 to 30 grams.

Pavement Punishments

Pavement in York is called thus because around 1329 it was the only clear piece of paved land in the centre of the city. Paving was unusual then. Before that Pavement was called Marketshire and was the site of markets (there once was a market cross here), proclamations and public punishments in days when the punishment was made, and seen, to fit the crime: for example, drunks were made to stand on barrels with pint pots on their heads and goose thieves were put in the stocks with goose wings draped unceremoniously around their necks.

Less amusingly, Catholic Thomas Percy, Earl of Northumberland, was beheaded at Pavement in front of All Saints church in 1572 for his opposition to Elizabeth I, in the Northern Rebellion which aimed to install Catholic Mary, Queen of Scots on the throne. The English paid the Scots a massive £2,000 to get him back to England, and specifically to the Catholic stronghold that was York. Despite efforts by the Pope and King Phillip of Spain to stop the execution, it went ahead. The beheading of Percy there was ideal propaganda and sent out a perfect message to any other would-be rebels. People from the seething crowd collected Percy's blood in their handkerchiefs and on their clothes as relics. His sword had been symbolically broken at nearby St. Crux Church and his torso taken there and buried in an unmarked grave. Percy's head ended up on Micklegate Bar and stayed there for two years whence it was taken to Holy Trinity in Goodramgate and buried.

Petty Treason

Petty treason or petit treason was an offence in English common law which involved the betrayal, including murder, of a superior by a subordinate. The element of betrayal explains why this crime was considered worse than an ordinary murder; at the time society depended on a foundation in which everyone had his or her appointed place and these murders were seen as threatening this foundation. Everyone almost had somebody subordinate to them and feared the consequences if the murder of superiors was not punished severely.

The common law offence was codified in the Treason Act 1351 in which petty treason was an aggravated form of murder. It consisted of:

- a wife killing her husband, this upset the 'natural hierarchy'.
- a clergyman killing his prelate or
- a servant killing his master or mistress, or his master's wife.

The Act automatically abolished three other forms of petty treason which had existed under common law:

- a wife attempting to kill her husband,
- a servant forging his master's seal, or
- a servant committing adultery with his master's wife or daughter.

The punishment for a woman convicted of petty treason was to be burned at the stake, but without being drawn there; the penalty for high treason was drawing and burning.

The law later offered some mercy to women who were to be thus executed: the executioner passed a cord around the victim's throat and would pull it tight, strangling her before the flames could reach her. It was not perfect, however, and there were instances of the cord burning through and the victim burning alive.

'Pleading the Belly'

The law did not allow the execution of pregnant women. When a woman was convicted of a capital crime, she would be asked if there was any reason why sentence of death should not be passed upon her. This is when she could "plead the belly", saying that she was pregnant. The woman was usually not sentenced to death at this point but kept in prison and examined by matrons to see if she really was pregnant. Many claims of pregnancy were entirely baseless. If, however, the woman was found by the panel of matrons to be "quick with child", (the foetus could be heard) her execution was delayed until after she had given birth or her sentence was commuted to transportation. If not, she was returned to court to be formally sentenced to death.

It comes as no surprise that some women prisoners would sometimes try to get pregnant while in prison to escape the gallows, offering sex to jailers or visitors. Mary Burgan is a case in point; she was released from York in 1710 under Queen Anne's general pardon when the jailer there, Thomas Ward, made her pregnant. The resulting son lived with Mary in York Castle, paid for by the state until he was ten years old when he left to take up an apprenticeship. In 1739 Naomi Hollings was to hang for burglary but avoided this by having a son whom she named Castellus after the Castle, his place of birth; Mary was later transported. The earliest case of belly pleading is in 1228; the plea was rendered obsolete by the Sentence of Death (Expectant Mothers) Act of 1931.

In Daniel Defoe's *Moll Flanders* (1721) one of the characters successfully pleads her belly despite 'being no more with child than the judge that tried [her]'; Flich in John Gay's *The Beggar's Opera* earns money as a 'child getter…helping the ladies to a pregnancy against their being called down to sentence'.

Prisons

TP Cooper in his 1911, *The History of the Castle of York*, gives us a fascinating glimpse of life in York Castle gaol; this extract is based on the inspections of John Howard (1726-1790) whose name, of course, lives on in the Howard League for Penal Reform.

'John Howard, a philanthropist who gave his life and energies to the reformation of the gigantic evils of the gaol system…He described in detail their noisome dungeons and the debased condition of the filthy and fever-haunted dens of iniquity, in which his fellow-citizens in festering masses were confined. His observations on the gaols of York are worth reprinting at this juncture, as we of the twentieth century have but a faint idea of the thoughtless and inhuman treatment of prisoners, and of the evils that existed in our prisons a little over a hundred years ago…". The felon's court is down five steps: it is too small, and has no water; the pump is just on the outside of the palisades. The day room for men is only 24 feet by 8; in it are three cells, in another place nine cells and three in another. The cells are in general about 7 feet by 6, and 8 high; close and dark, having only either a hole over the door about 4 inches by 8, or some perforations in the door of about an inch in diameter, not any of them to the open air but into passages or entries. In most of these cells three prisoners are locked up at night; in winter from four-teen to sixteen hours; straw on the stone floors, no bedsteads. There are four condemned rooms about 7 feet square. A sewer in one of the passages often makes these parts of the gaol very offensive, and I cannot say they are clean. Indeed a clean prison is scarcely ever seen… The prisoners are allowed one pound and a half of wheaten bread daily, and one shilling per week … Through this grating they [felons] keep up a free and easy communication, not only with the debtors but with the public. At this very time a great number of persons were standing at the outside, holding conversation with the prisoners. Men and women, grown-up persons and children, have an equal access to this scene of depravity and distress. It is evident that so free a communication must give every facility to the introduction of improper articles into the prison, and probably to the pawning of the prisoners' clothes, which we under- stand to be a prevalent custom here; it must also afford an easy opportunity of corruption to the inhabitants of York and its neighbourhood'.

The Resurrection Men or Jerry Crunchers

Bodysnatching is the clandestine disinterment of corpses from graveyards or other places of burial. It is inextricably associated with murder. Good money could be earned from bodysnatching because the usual purpose of snatching a body, especially in the 19th century, was to sell it for dissection for anatomy and physiology lectures to medical schools. The examination of corpses also provided good training for surgeons who may have to perform amputations and other procedures.

Prior to the Anatomy Act of 1832, the only legal supply of corpses for medical school preclinical training in the UK were those of criminals condemned to death and dissection, often criminals found guilty of the harsher crimes. This supply was woefully inadequate to satisfy the needs of the many medical schools and private anatomical schools which did not require a licence before 1832. During the 18th century hundreds of criminals had been executed for relatively trivial crimes, but by the 19th century on average only about 55 people were given capital punishment each year. The expansion of the medical schools, however, meant that 500 cadavers were needed annually.

Tampering with a grave was a misdemeanour at common law, not a felony, so punishable with a fine and or imprisonment rather than transportation or execution. The rewards were good enough to risk being caught, particularly as many authorities turned a blind eye to what they considered a necessary evil.

To help deter this infernal trade, relatives and friends of the recently deceased would stand sentinel over a body until burial, and then guard the grave after burial, to stop it being raided. Iron coffins were often used, and graves were protected by fenceworks made of iron bars and called mortsafes. Mort houses were also used to store bodies until decomposition had taken place when the cadavers were quite useless for medical dissection.

The best way to snatch a body was to dig down at the head end of a fresh burial, using a wooden spade which was less noisy than metal, and, on reaching the coffin, break it open and loop a rope around the corpse and drag it out. The jerry snatcher would be very careful not to steal any jewellery or clothes as this would render him liable to a felony charge, and the transportation or execution that went with it – even ending up on the dissection table himself.

The Lancet in 1896 revealed another method. A square of turf was removed 15 to 20 feet away from the head of the grave, and a tunnel dug to the coffin, which would be about 4 feet under the ground. The end of the coffin would be wrenched off, and the corpse pulled up through the tunnel. The turf was then replaced; any relatives guarding the graves would not usually notice any disturbance. *The Lancet* concludes that the sheer number of empty coffins found "proves beyond a doubt that at this time body snatching was frequent".

Instances of bodysnatching and burking (after Burke and Hare where victims are murdered for their cadavers) abounded in Yorkshire and in particular in York – partly because the city was on the main coach route to Edinburgh and its famous medical school. Even after the passing of the Anatomy Act which legalised the trafficking of the bodies of lunatics and paupers between Poor Law Unions and medical schools, the 'unhallowed occupation' continued here – probably due to the opening of York's first medical school. *The York Courant* of January 14th 1834 reports one case of bodysnatching when in St Saviourgate 'one Matthew Joy when questioned…stated that he merely wanted a skull for a person who had applied to him for one, in order to pulverise it, and mix it with some treacle, to give it to a person who was subject to fits'.

Laurence Sterne (1713-1768) is famous for his *The Life and Opinions of Tristram Shandy, Gentleman*, and *A Sentimental Journey Through France and Italy*; he was also an Anglican clergyman with a vicarship at Sutton-on-the-Forest, a living at Stillington and was a prebendary of York Minster, lodging at Hildyard's in Stonegate. Sterne died of pleurisy in London in 1768; he is now buried in the churchyard in Coxwold, but only after a circuitous journey… having been originally interred in St. George's Churchyard, Hanover Square, London. His body was snatched by 'resurrection men' for use in medical dissection at Cambridge University. The cadaver was recognised by the Professor of Anatomy there who fainted when he saw it on the table and had it hastily reburied. In 1969 the Lawrence Sterne Society obtained permission to remove Sterne's remains to Coxwold for re-burial .

Strychnine

Poison berry, *nux vomica*, strychnine was well known for its medicinal qualities usually in the form of St Ignatius's Bean which contained 1% of strychnine and came from India's Malabar Coast. It was used to reduce fever, and, more controversially, to adulterate beer by the brewers around 1852. The poisoner only needed to administer one third of a grain by mouth to achieve the desired effect: the first symptom is *risus sardonicus* – a grin – followed by a spasm, continuous convulsions until the backbone arches, and *trismus* (lockjaw). There is no specific antidote for strychnine.

Terry's and the Edinburgh Poison Case 1941

In 1941, Terry's of York was embroiled in the Edinburgh Poison Case when a disaffected Brigadier General Tredegar (actually John Millar) attempted to poison Georgina Ferguson with a box of Terry's Devon Milk laced with toxic permanganate of potash and sent through the post to her. He was duly convicted of attempted murder and sentenced to three year's penal servitude.

Stephen Wade (1887-1956)

A Doncaster hangman on the Home Office List between 1940 and 1955. Stephen Wade first applied for a hanging post when he left the army in 1918, aged 21. He was deemed to be too young but persisted and finally made it onto the list in 1940. After assisting both Tom and Albert Pierrepoint he finally got to be the No. 1 at the execution of Arthur Charles at Durham on 26th March 1946.

Women and Murder

Murder was far and away the most common crime for which women were hanged in the 19th century, no less than 78.6% of the total number of women executed which amounts to 142 women hanged for this crime. A further twenty were hanged for the murder of a bastard child, defined as a separate crime from ordinary murder. Three women were executed for attempted murder, and one each for being an accessory to murder, one for conspiracy to murder and one for aiding and abetting murder.

Women convicted of murdering their husbands (at least eighteen cases) and superiors (for example their employers) before 1828, were guilty of petty treason and were dragged to the gallows on a sledge before being hanged. An example is Martha Aldin who had murdered her husband: on "Friday next you will be drawn on a hurdle to the place of execution, there to be hanged by the neck till you are dead, and your body afterwards to be dissected". The sentence was carried out in full on 31st July 1807, at 12 noon, before a large crowd on Castle Hill, Norwich. Thirty-one women were executed for petty treason.

Between 1735 and 1799 around 1,600 women and girls were sentenced to death in England and Wales. Of these, at least 355 were executed, 323 by hanging and 32 by burning at the stake. At least 1,230 were reprieved, giving a reprieve rate of 78%. Of the executions 187 were for murder, 52.7% of the total. Eighty of these were hanged for the murder of their bastard child. Who knows how many of these babies were stillborn or died of natural causes soon after birth?

Here is the York death toll:

- Monday 28th March 1757 Mary Ellah of Broomfleet burned for petty treason for the murder of husband, Thomas with an axe blow to his head.

- Monday 10th August 1767 Ann Sowerby burned for petty treason for the murder of her husband, Timothy by poison, nux vomica and arsenic.

- Wednesday 20th March 1776 Elizabeth Boardingham with one man burned for petty treason for the murder of husband, John; co-accused Thomas Aikney hanged with her. She was the last women to be burned at York.

- Monday 22nd March 1784 Lydia Dickenson hanged for murder of her female bastard.

- Saturday 5th April 1788 Catherine Savage hanged with six men for burglary.

- Monday 3rd August 1789 Hannah Whitley hanged for the murder of Joseph Rhodes with arsenic in a pie.

- Monday 26th March 1792 Elizabeth Elliot hanged for the murder of Mary Walker.

- Tuesday 12th August 1794 Ann Scalberd hanged for the murder of her mother-in-law, Mary Scalberd.